CONTENTS

———————————— Continued on next page ————————————

Continued from previous page

Soundings

Issue 8

Active
Welfare

EDITORS
Stuart Hall
Doreen Massey
Michael Rustin

GUEST EDITORS
Andrew Cooper
Rachael Hetherington
Helen Morgan

POETRY EDITOR
Carole Satyamurti

REVIEWS EDITORS
Becky Hall and
Susanna Rustin

ART EDITOR
Tim Davison

EDITORIAL OFFICE
Lawrence & Wishart
99a Wallis Road
London E9 5LN

MARKETING CONSULTANT
Mark Perryman

ADVERTISEMENTS
Write for information to Soundings,
c/o Lawrence & Wishart

SUBSCRIPTIONS
1998 subscription rates are (for three issues):
UK: Institutions £70, Individuals £35
Rest of the world: Institutions £80, Individuals £45

ISSN 1362 6620
ISBN 0 85315 869 X

Text setting Art Services, Norwich
Cover photograph: © David Gibson

Printed in Great Britain by
Cambridge University Press, Cambridge

Soundings is published three
times a year, in autumn,
spring and summer by:
Soundings Ltd
c/o Lawrence & Wishart
99a Wallis Road
London E9 5LN

NOTES ON CONTRIBUTORS

Manfred Pfister is Professor of English Literature at the Free University of Berlin. He is one of the editors of *The Journal for the Study of British Cultures*, which is published in Tubingen.

Patrick Wright is the author of *On Living in an Old Country; the National Past in Contemporary Britain* (Verso, 1985) and *A Journey Through Ruins* (Radius, 1991). His latest book is *The Village that Died for England; the Strange Story of Tyneham* (Cape, 1995).

John Strawson teaches Law and Middle Eastern studies at the University of East London and works with the Birzeit Law Centre in Palestine.

Catherine Byron teaches at Nottingham Trent University. Her latest collection of poetry is *The Fat-Hen Field Hospital* (1993).

Jane Evans was born in 1933 and wrote poems from an early age. She is a teacher of children with hearing difficulties.

Frances Angela has worked as a photographer and in mental health.

U.A. Fanthorpe's most recent collection of poetry, *Safe as Houses*, was published in 1995. A Penguin Audiobook, *Double Act* (with R.V. Bailey) appeared in 1997.

Gregory Warren Watson is a professional violinist. His latest collection of poetry is *Hanging Windchimes in a Vacuum* (1997).

Colette Harris is based at the Institute of Development Research of the University of Amsterdam and is co-ordinating a women's health-education project in rural Tajikistan.

Michael Rustin is joint editor of *Soundings*.

Rebecca L. Walkowitz is a doctoral student in the Department of English at Harvard University, where she is writing a dissertation on cosmopolitanism and the modern novel.

Paul Myerscough is a tutor at the University of Sussex, and is currently researching representations of collective madness.

Reina Lewis teaches in the Department of Cultural Studies at the University of East London. She is author of *Gendering Orientalism: Race, Femininity and Representation* (Routledge, 1996) and co-editor of *Outlooks: Lesbian and Gay Sexualities and Visual Culture* (Routledge, 1996).

Joanna Clarke-Jones works as a journalist on the *Camden New Journal*.

Andrew Cooper is Professor of Social Work at the Tavistock Clinic and University of East London. In recent years he has worked with Rachael Hetherington and others on a number of comparative studies of European child protection systems and practices. He was a co-convenor of the ESRC research seminars out of which the *Active Welfare* Special Issue of *Soundings* emerged.

Rachael Hetherington is Director of the Centre for Comparative Social Work Studies at Brunel University. Her main research interest is in the comparative study of social work practices in Europe. Currently she is engaged in a project comparing the nature of co-operation between services for child protection and for community mental health in several European countries.

Helen Morgan is a full Member of the British Association of Psychotherapists. Her background is in mental health work and she is currently a self-employed psychotherapist, consultant and trainer.

Alain Grevot is Director of the Beauvais office of *Jeunesse Culture Loisirs Technique (JSLT)* and of the organisation's national research centre in Paris.

Hassan Ezzedine is an *Educateur Specialise* working in a JCLT prevention team in Beauvais in northern France.

John Pitts is Professor of Socio-legal studies at the Vauxhall Centre for the Study of Crime at the University of Luton. He is currently engaged in research into inter-racial violence and youth justice in an inner London borough, and has been involved in Anglo-French studies of child protection and youth crime and justice.

Angela Leopold received her B.A. in Sociology from Gothenburg University in Sweden. Subsequently she lived in the United States, where she became a potter, and also in Italy. In 1988 she returned to Sweden where she is now employed in social work.

Monica Savio is a sociologist by training; she has a Ph.D in Social Science and Administration from the London School of Economics, and specialises in comparative social psychiatry. She is a consultant at the Department of Mental Health in Pordenone and works as a trainer and organisational consultant in the mental health private and public sectors.

Angelo Cassin is a consultant psychiatrist and Director of the Department of Mental Health in Pordenone, in North Italy.

Margherita Gobbi is a psychologist and psychoanalyst. She is both a clinical practitioner and a trainer in the mental health field, specialising in the treatment of people with a diagnosis of psychosis. She currently acts as the Director of the Training and Research Department in the Department of Mental Health in Pordenone, North Italy.

The New Labour project

Soundings began only a year or so before Labour took office, and this political transition unavoidably sets a significant part of our agenda. Even though we have always argued that Whitehall and Westminster are not all there is to politics, there is no doubting the importance of what the new government does and plans to do.

What is the New Labour project? We think it is important to represent this truthfully, in terms with which its own exponents might not quarrel unduly. It is a common failing of New Labour to define itself largely by antithesis with an under-specified set of beliefs conveniently labelled Old Labour. There is no point in our repeating this practice in reverse. The Blair project is, we believe, based on a coherent view of the contemporary world and of the possibilities for a reforming politics within it. Unless this project is understood, in both its strengths and weaknesses, it is impossible to develop any critical engagement with it.

The fundamental assumption of the Blair project is that unless Britain can reach the standard of performance of its global competitors, in virtually every aspect of life, there is no hope of achieving lasting improvements in well-being. 'Getting competitive' is the name of its game. This frame of thinking is shaping most fields of government policy. It is why New Labour seems so to admire successful businesspeople, has brought them into government, and has been appointing them to sort out struggling public institutions. Much more radically (since all governments seek good relations with business) is the way that this 'get competitive' idea is shaping the government's relationship with all its citizens.

The reason for the government's rejection of traditional programmes of redistribution, of increased benefits to the poor, is the view that improvements in living standards achieved by such means are bound to be trivial and shortlived. Only if individuals are helped to help themselves, in particular into the labour market and into higher-skilled work, can any difference be made. This is the logic of welfare-to-work, of pushing single parents into the labour market, and no doubt soon of a social security reform which in one way or another will encourage greater self-reliance and self-provision. The aim is to remoralise the labour force, and to lower expectations of what can be expected as social entitlements. There seems to be an intolerance of all dependency.

This competition agenda also dominates the government's education policy. Competitive norms are setting the goals, (what Japanese children can achieve in mathematics, British children should be able to do), and also the means for achieving those goals (league tables, sanctions for underperforming schools and teachers). There is to be little shelter from the competitive winds, except for those who can indisputably demonstrate that they are incapable, and new thinking about disability benefit shows that this is going to be made harder to do. And those who are not merely dependent, but also delinquent, or whose children are delinquent, will be subject to stricter compulsion and where necessary punishment - for example, the parents of truanting children.

Even the constitutional reforms espoused by the new government probably form part of the 'competitiveness' agenda, though they are widely understood in other terms. The common radical view is that this is the one area where *real* changes are being promoted, in ways which are apparently in contradiction with the rest of the minimal programme. But whilst one welcomes the prospect of new political spaces being opened up, by devolution for example, it is worth asking how the Blairites themselves regard these reforms, and how they reconcile them with what are plainly their dominant goals.

It is possible that the purpose of creating a measure of devolution is to establish sub-national and regional governments which will become more, and not less, responsive to the imperatives of competitiveness. A Labour-dominated devolved government in Scotland can, after all, be expected to have more legitimacy than the Conservatives ever had there, to preach the doctrines of economic, and welfare, realism. Scotland and Wales may well have to pay in their share of UK public expenditure for the privilege of self-rule. 'Mayors in every large city', which Tony Blair is reported to favour, will be expected to be more effective agents of 'partnership' with business enterprise than majority groups on Labour councils have habitually been. It seems likely that New Labour regards its constitutional reforms more as part of its contribution to its own version of enterprise culture, than as its antithesis or corrective.

The Millennium Dome is being constructed as a symbol of this governing philosophy. It is presently the centrepiece of the strategy, recommended by Demos, of 'rebranding Britain', but is likely to display all the contradictions that might be expected from the assertion of British national identity at a moment of its general crisis, both internal and external.

This is all, in sum, a programme to re-shape the national psyche, in the people's own self-interest. This is a process of 'individualisation' viewed not merely as the outcome of larger social trends - increased mobility, communication, the informational revolution - but as a positive strategy of competitive survival. It is a Foucauldian dream of governing the soul, broadcast from Downing Street. The continuities with Thatcherism, with its earlier attacks on the 'dependency culture', on collectivism, and on values which seemed hostile to the market, are undeniable. Peter Mandelson and Roger Liddell, in their valuable outline of the New Labour agenda, did say after all that there were many things which Thatcher got right.

The exponents of this strategy appear to be in good faith in their belief that this programme is the only one which can advance the interests of *all* the people, including the weakest. It is not, in its conscious purpose at least, merely meant as a means to reward the successful. The Blairites pride themselves on their realism, on the idea that one can do nothing without confronting the world as it is. It was such a view that made them into such formidable election-winners, and makes them see the political process (as we explored in *Soundings* 4) as an instrumental one meant almost exclusively for the capture and effective use of power.

But is 'getting competitive', on a New Labour basis, the only possible form of realism? There are considerable reasons for thinking not.

One problem in establishing any kind of constructive dialogue with New Labour is the reluctance of its exponents to engage in much thinking aloud. The imperatives of short-term advantage - the macho virtues of decisiveness, absolute certainty, and dynamism - have been winning hands-down over any possible benefits of a more open debate about larger strategic assumptions and objectives. (Sarah Benton, in *Soundings* 5 and *Special*, has described the dominance of mythical registers over rational ones in New Labour's discourse.) Sound-bites substitute for thought. It seems likely that, as with Thatcherism, mainly tactical advantages are being sought by this method of approach. It was Thatcherism's opponents, after all, who were left with the task of analysing the logic of the larger strategy, whilst the Thatcherites appeared to proceed in a merely incremental way, new ideas (e.g. privatisation) arriving unannounced as they went along. It may indeed be a logic of unintended but inevitable consequences which propels such transformations, not a pre-conceived plan. 'Good faith' (in the values of social justice, opportunities, social cohesion, social justice) may only be preserved by *not* thinking too far ahead, and 'good faith', as Tony Blair's every public appearance reminds us, is his project's most crucial political resource.

One major theoretical argument underlies New Labour's approach, which is made more and not less influential by the fact that it remains largely implicit. This is a particular version of globalisation theory, seen as a process which now exposes the entire world to market pressures which can only be successfully responded to in terms of enhanced competitiveness. The main role assigned to government in this scenario is as agent of this process. Globalisation is another term for market forces operating on an international plane. Their effect is felt in the constraints upon governments to accept the prevailing 'rules of the game' as financial markets dictate them, in the necessity to adapt to the investment priorities of business corporations, whatever these are; and in the irrelevance and indeed retrograde harmfulness of all conceptions of value or motive which might lead anyone to neglect or defy this reality.

Adaptation to this 'real world' is primarily viewed as a matter for individuals. This has always been the prevalent Anglo-Saxon attitude, and the current crisis of the 'Asian Tigers' - induced in part by the neo-liberal IMF - and the sluggishness of the continental European economies as they mortify themselves to enter a European Monetary Union built on the same principles - is undermining the challenge to it from a more 'social' model. Impersonal flows of money on the one hand, individuals mobilised by a new enterprise culture on the other - this seems to be the social geography imagined by New Labour. It adopts the negative half of the argument developed by Manuel Castells in his major trilogy, *The Information Age* - about the power of global capital in the informational revolution - and ignores both his critique of its hugely divisive effects, and his positive argument that new social identities and values can and will create themselves in order to wrest human control from this impersonal engine of transformation.

It is a notable and defining fact about 'New Labour' that for the first time the power of capital and the markets which empower it is regarded as merely a fact of life, a reality to be accommodated to, and not a problem, a force to be questioned and resisted. The abstractions of 'globalisation', 'individualisation', even 'informationalism', can be used to reify the real agents and interests which dominate the contemporary world. New Labour has uncritically adopted a partial version of a complex argument. Analyses of 'globalisation' which we have already published (by Paul Hirst and Grahame Thompson in *Soundings* 4, by David Goldblatt, David Held and colleagues in *No 7*, and in Doreen Massey's editorial in the same issue) question these assumptions, and seek to reinterpret 'globalisation' as a process potentially subject to democratic intervention.

There are two critical questions which can be asked about New Labour's assumptions. One, will 'competitiveness' be achieved by the programme being adopted? Is 'competitiveness' not as often the outcome of institutional, cultural and collective resources, as of individual drives? We think government should be identifying as the main agents of development a variety of institutions and social agencies, and should be seeking ways of mobilising *their* capabilities. (Ash Amin explored this model in our *Special Issue.*) This would be the 'stakeholder agenda', taken seriously, since it requires enhancing obligations (e.g. of the owners of capital to those they employ, supply, and work among, to the environment and future generations), and establishing in public institutions more active means of social accountability. Models of welfare institutions which operate in more participatory ways have been explored in both our *Public Good* and this *Active Welfare* issue. A climate of punitive audit, public shaming, and scapegoating, such as current policy is evoking in order to coerce providers such as teachers, will not have good general outcomes, since damage done to morale, confidence and cooperative work will outweigh any local benefits. The improvements of some, in such an atmosphere, are won at the expense of the demoralisation of the many.

The second critical question to ask is at what cost is 'competitiveness' made into the overriding goal? Does nothing else matter, than Gross National Product and aggregate levels of consumption? One example is the new policy towards single parents. Granted, access to the labour market can be a positive benefit in many ways. But how is it that no discrimination is even being made between the needs of infants and pre-school children, for whom care at home may reasonably be chosen by parents as a preferred option, and the needs of children over four or five, who are in full-time school? Why should the needs of the labour market rule over all other considerations? (In this case, probably because of an American-inspired vicious myth of 'welfare mothers', conceiving children in order to scrounge off the state, which however no-one quite dares to admit to believing.)

The problem is that a nation which is on the face of it highly 'competitive' in economic terms can be at the same time a most unjust and oppressive social order. The United States, the implicit model for much though not all of New Labour's agenda (they did after all ban handguns soon after the election), is the paradigm instance of the non-correlation of wealth and well-being. A more competitive society, in aggregate terms, may turn out to be a more unequal one, and a less unequal one less competitive, in certain respects. Some in the New Labour leadership seem to see this as an unavoidable trade-off, and it may be this belief that competitiveness has to be achieved even at the expense of greater inequality which underpins the commitment not to increase income taxes on the rich.

Richard Wilkinson's article in our *Next Ten Years* issue advanced a different view. Well-being, he argued, extrapolating from data on the incidence of health and illness, is affected adversely by inequality. In more unequal societies, there is more illness and lower life-expectancy, on average and not just for the worse-off. What causes this seems to be the 'hidden injuries' of relative failure and the anxiety which this brings. It is competitiveness, where basic guarantees and respect are not provided for all, which does the damage. The ambiguity of the idea of 'competitiveness' - does it mean a nation which competes more, or individual citizens who are forced to compete more with each other? - emerges as a central issue. For New Labour, it seems clear that competitiveness has become an objective in both these senses.

For *Soundings*, markets, globalisation, and individualisation, are outcomes of social choices, and of unequal divisions of power. If the democratic state, both nationally, and on a larger scale, has any useful function, it is to influence these decisions, and at the least provide some counterbalance to irresponsible powers such as those which are mediated through global markets.

It is vital that arguments of this sort be heard within the New Labour system, if the government is to become more than merely an instrument of adaptation to global market forces. We hope that there are some who want the government to be more than the executive arm of 'Britain plc', and that they will contribute to debate about a more complex conception of a 'modernised Britain'.

In all this, public dialogue is fundamental. If democratic publics are to have effective access to decision-making - this is what citizenship should mean - the assumptions and beliefs underlying decisions must be made clear. New Labour would make a major contribution to its own development, as a project, and to its proclaimed development of a 'new Britain', if it found the confidence to tell the rest of us what its long-term perspectives are, so that these can be explored in a rational spirit.

MJR

Writing the obituaries

Manfred Pfister *talks to* Patrick Wright

Each Britain gets the (re-)discoverers it deserves. For Thatcher's and post-Thatcher Britain, one of them, and perhaps the most intrepid, is Patrick Wright. His particular field of exploration lies where two opposing forces crosshatch each other to create tensions and paradoxes: on the one hand, the fiercely modernising thrust of a new market economy dismantling the ethos and structures of the Welfare State, together with traditional ways of living and thinking; on the other, the resurgence of ecological and cultural conservationism and the recycling of British history in a new heritage industry.

His three books so far explore these tensions and paradoxes in different places and, together, form a trilogy on a Britain that is decidedly no longer 'Great'. On Living in an Old Country; the National Past in Contemporary Britain (Verso 1985) is a series of interconnected essays and stories on the political uses of nostalgia, revolving round the central story of the triumphal recovery, in 1982, of the 'Mary Rose', Henry VIII's flagship that had lain in the bed of the Solent for more than four centuries, and its coincidence with Thatcher's triumph over the Falklands in the South Atlantic. 'The Falklands adventure made a new combination possible: this small war enabled Thatcher to draw up the legitimising traditions of the "nation" around a completely unameliorated 'modernising' monetarist programme. This new and charismatic style of legitimisation fused a valorisation of national tradition and identity with a policy and programme which is fundamentally destructive of the customary ways and values to which it appeals.' (186) Other stories, some of them bordering on the bizarre, focus upon the commodification of national heritage and the English countryside as, for instance, in Shell's advertisement campaigns that have linked motoring with the appeal to 'Discover Britain', or upon attempts to save historical heirlooms from destruction that range from institutions like the National Trust to quixotic individual initiatives like Miss Savidge's whoelsale removal of her Tudor home from Hertfordshire to Norfolk.

A Journey Through Ruins (*Radius* 1991), dedicated to Lady Margaret Thatcher, is brilliantly misnamed: there is very little journeying going on in the book, which preserves a classical unity of place in exploring the 'Condition of England' by focussing on one part of it - London's East End or, more specifically, Hackney or, even more specifically, Dalston Lane. This epitome of Britain suffices for this in-depth explorer to study the history of the post-war Welfare State in terms of the rise and fall of the tower blocks and the coversion of Victorian 'hell-houses' into luxury flats. The trope that unifies this travelogue en miniature is architecture: the fortunes of buildings lost or perserved - buildings as small as Sir Giles Gilbert Scott's red telephone boxes or as large as tower blocks and country houses - of streets that change under the impact of a new multi-ethnic population, or of whole areas for which gentrification re-invents historical roots. This involves a critical engagement with the various conflicting discourses of architecture and urban planning and their political implications - most notably with Prince Charles' indictments of an un-English modernism in which, once again, conservationism and a revivalist 'Vision of Britain' is shown to be linked up with a rejection of values that are part of the very Great Tradition to which it appeals.

In his most recent book, The Village that Died for England; the Strange Story of Tyneham (*Cape* 1995) Wright moves from the town to the country. This move does not, however, come as a complete surprise. A Journey Through Ruins has already built a number of thematic bridgeheads for it: country houses and the ambivalences of their conservation and celebration, telephone boxes ancient and modern, or metal detecting which, in its anarchichally individualistic archaeology, provides an apt metaphor for the author's own detection and discoveries. Here, for once, Wright tells one story - the story of how Tyneham, the picturesque, even Arcadian village on one of the most beautiful stretches of the Dorset coast, was destroyed by the advent of tanks, for which this remote area of Hardy's Wessex has proved an ideal testing ground and gunnery range ever since the Great War. This one story explodes, however, into an intricate maze of stories as it is mainly told in terms of the responses it has elicited *locally and nationally. What is at stake here is, again, conservation - the conservation both of historical monuments, traditional lifestyles and the natural environment - and again the issue of conservationism is made to function as a magnifying glass that focusses the wider political or ideological conflicts and contradictions of twentieth century Britain.*

(MP)

This interview is part of an intellectual project to delineate for the first time the history of the British touring, mapping and describing of their own country in non-fictional texts.[1] These texts have, for half a millennium, contributed vitally to constructing a sense of identity for England or Great Britain that goes beyond the merely geographical. We have chosen the metaphor of 'discovery' to highlight the fact that the discovery of the new worlds beyond the Atlantic actually coincided with the first attempts by British cartographers and chorographers systematically to explore and describe their own country in its entirety: both projects started in the sixteenth century, you could say, and both were tied up with a new sense of national identity.

Yes, this is true; and all sorts of more aesthetic conventions of internal travel and observation were produced in the same process. So I agree with you. There seems to be a coupling in which the discovery and colonisation of distant domains comes to be combined with an often very fanciful 'discovery' of what Britain itself may be.

So you find the metaphor of 'discovery' of Britain helpful? It is a metaphor after all ...

A metaphor yes, but one that is historically justified, since many of the observers who have made these interior journeys into Britain have explicitly presented themselves as 'discoverers'. If the metaphor has value, it is partly because it reveals the artifice involved in the process it describes. Plainly, we are talking about a rhetorical strategy rather than a literal process of discovery. This is true whether one is thinking about those eighteenth century travellers who

---

1. This interview is based on a conversation recorded in London in January 1997, and was prepared for a special issue, *The Discovery of Britain*, of *The Journal for the Study of British Cultures*, Berlin 1997 (Vol 4 No1-2/97).

'discovered' the picturesque in places like the Lake District and the Vale of Festiniog in Wales, or those more recent internal voyagers who have set out to 'discover' the inner city deprivations of East London, unemployment on Glaswegian housing estates, or the Kashmiri world of Bradford. Like other literary conventions, this one is fairly pliable: Britain has been 'discovered' from diverse and often contrary points of view. The results of the 'discovery' can be used in very different ways too. I'm interested in the way a particular 'discovered' construction of Britain, and perhaps especially of England, was used as a kind of schoolhouse device all over the British Empire. If you look at what was being taught in Caribbean church schools in the 1920s or even the 1950s, it's as if Beatrix Potter's Flopsy Bunny and Jemima Puddleduck and all that stuff was still running. Many people who later came to Britain as immigrants, discovered what it is like to arrive in a country that is wildly out of harmony with its own carefully fostered overseas image.

We actually have one essay on that particular topic in our collection, Tobias Doring's 'The Empire is travelling back' contrasting such expectations with first-hand experience.

So I think this metaphor of 'discovery' is a potent one, but I also think that once you have said 'discovery' you have to move on pretty fast to consider the context, and ask, well, by whom, where and why, and at what time and with what results? And then one sees that the most beautiful or evocative aspects of discovered England are often tinged with fairly morbid contents, so that, for example, the most innocuous pastoral celebration of ancient continuities in the landscape may be, not just historically false, but functionally exclusive in the present. Leafy green England was an inspiration for nineteenth century socialists, but it is also held most dear by people who can't stand immigrants. These patterns are part of the story as well.

Such discoveries or their descriptions are, indeed, rarely innocent.

I agree, and yet they are not always entirely guilty either. One of the things that I was most interested to discover while writing my last book, *The Village that Died for England*, was that throughout the twentieth century there is this tradition of people going out into the rural areas and trying to discover an England of connectedness: not of picturesque views, not of landscape reduced to a scenic resource for urban visitors, but an England of local vitality, which was still in touch with the traditions of the yeomanry and peasantry, with crafts and pre-enclosure land rights too. Throughout the 1920s and 1930s there was an increasingly desperate pursuit of relics, rural relics, which seemed to tell the story of an industrious, independent and almost Guild Socialist type of rural life - something that William Morris would have recognised and approved of. Once you start looking at this, and its battle with a rising urban and touristic rural aesthetic, you realise that one 'discovery' can be very much in conflict with another.

Of course there is a lineage too of one traveller 'citing' the place that the last one went to. For a radio programme, I recently talked to Richard Holmes, the biographer of Coleridge. He has walked the parts of the west country where Coleridge wrote many of his poems, and has discovered the routes that are implicit in the development of the narrative and metrical patterns of some of his best poems. Holmes was describing how he found a cave that Coleridge had mentioned and, with great excitement, discovered the letters 'S.T.C.' carved in the stone. A moment later he realised that the inscription was recent, carved by another admirer who had gone there before him. So there are these artificial traditions of initials reinscribed on oak trees and limestone, which are part of the history as well.

You yourself don't use the metaphor of discovery that much. The metaphors you use are metaphors of archaeology, rather, or even of metal detection - you dig beneath the surface.

The metaphor of discovery strikes me as easily overdone: it belongs in a tradition that I would prefer to assess critically rather than simply sign up to. An imperial explorer like Livingstone could go into darkest Africa and discover things that were then brought into modern colonial administration, albeit often with dire consequences. But to pretend that a literary explorer can do anything similar in Britain is feeble really - at best an ironically reversed imperial convention, and more likely the last resort of the voyeuristic 'travel writer' who can't afford an air ticket, and who certainly couldn't administer even a bad colonial health programme. The metaphor is not one that I would use in the present, because I think modern society confounds simple 'discovery'. What you find is complexity, tensions and this imploded imperial imagery, which Britons both love and hate. I do write about place, but I'm not taken by the idea of a country to be 'encountered' in the style of darkest Africa, or to be surveyed and then mapped from a single and superior point of view - even if the superiority is only presented now as outsiderish wit, as it often is by writers like Bryson and Theroux. I feel more at home with the idea of a *territory* where various interests and forces are in movement - often far from local and sometimes hidden deep beneath the immediate surface of things - and where economic, cultural and political forces meet in ways that can seem both accidental and revealing. So I suppose I do have a conception that is more archaeological.

I can tell you how I came into this though. In 1970, I went to the University of Kent, which was a new university, founded five years previously and still shining on its hillside overlooking Canterbury cathedral. There was a lot of concrete and glass, and endless construction work too. The campus could hardly even boast a bush in those days; they had only just planted the trees. The first thing any student of the humanities was asked to do on arriving was to read Thomas Mann's *The Magic Mountain,* a great novel set in an isolated tuberculosis clinic high up in the Swiss Alps, and with hundreds of pages devoted to vast philosophical arguments, many of them the founding debates of twentieth century thought. That's how we began in this new university where everything seemed absolutely contemporary - including the curriculum, which was interdisciplinary, modernist and, so I understand, more culturally ambitious than it is nowadays.

I graduated in 1973, and didn't really know what to do. Those new universities were profoundly disconnected in their early days: no Oxbridge style old boy network, even for those who wanted to use it, and the distances had been widened by much publicised incidents of student rebellion etc. The country was all but immobilised by industrial disputes and the oil crisis, and those of us who had entertained vague counter-cultural dreams of getting by on what used to be called 'the squatting/dole nexus', were having to wake up fast. As a student, I may have spent a lot of time gazing down through plate glass at Canterbury Cathedral, but Britain then was not a tranquil or dreamy place you might want to write travel books about. I had to make a decision about how to get by, how to make a living. I did a bit of school teaching, but quickly felt trapped. So I fled, I mean I left and went to the west coast, where I had friends. First California, and then Vancouver in Canada, a place where the 1960s seemed to struggle on for longer than elsewhere. I did the longest masters degree ever. It took me five years in all, but then I always knew that when I was finished - when the visa ran out - I would have to return to Britain.

What was your dissertation project about?

I was writing about the literary modernists, about those people who were in London before and during the Great War, particularly the American Imagist poet H.D., who later visited Vienna to go through a brief analysis with Freud. So there was a project of sorts there, but at the same time I was in British Columbia, a province that is now much more clearly orientated across the Pacific, but was then still full of colonial British residues. You could go to a place called Victoria, a small city on Vancouver Island, where there was a hotel called 'The Empress' where people were still sipping afternoon tea in a Victorian manner that bore no relationship to the England I had grown up in. There was no connection between this frozen expatriate dream of England and the crisis-ridden country I had just left. So I saw a staged version of Englishness, which consisted almost entirely of clichés, of red telephone boxes, regattas and tea ceremonies which rivalled the Japanese for ritual. There was also this fading assumption that if you came from Britain you were OK - especially if you came from a time before the recent decline! There were some exceptions, but the universities I attended had more than their fair share of mediocre British academics - characters who hadn't been able to get a job in Britain and who despised themselves for being there and also their 'dumb colonial' students. I made the decision, which was mixed up with the usual personal confusions, that I didn't want to be a Briton in Canada.

So I came back to England with the old problem of how to make a living still unresolved. I returned in 1979; it must have been summer 1979. And I had to make sense both of the country I had returned to and of my own distanced familiarity with it. These layers of confusion were the starting point for the writing I went on to do. I got back just in time for my return to coincide with Margaret Thatcher's election as Prime Minister. And the minute she took over the cuts on the higher education system began in earnest. So I found myself sort of structurally unemployable. I mean, I never taught in a university and my first book, *On Living in an Old Country*, started out as an orphaned Ph.D. thesis. I was registered for a year at the Centre for Contemporary Cultural Studies at Birmingham University, but I couldn't raise the fees to continue.

You taught at polytechnics didn't you?

Well, I taught very briefly.

And in one of your few autobiographical digressions, I think it is in A Journey Through Ruins *(pp42-46), you give us a brief account of ...*

...of falling out of the bottom of that system too. It's quite true. I managed to get a one-term part-time teaching job at a polytechnic in Coventry, teaching media studies in a department of art historians. Many of them loathed the very idea of media studies, but they were desperate for students, so they started this course that they were not actually willing or able to teach. I joined the list of casualised visitors who were drafted in to run it on a short-term basis. Perhaps I had made the great leap up to the bottom rung of the teaching ladder, but when I looked up all I saw was Keith Joseph, Thatcher's education minister, sawing it off with a mad look in his eye. So I let go, and I ended up teaching literacy around the country. I mean, I spent a year teaching people how to write business reports. I used to teach secretaries letter writing, and mining engineers how to do public speaking.

So you taught remedial English?

Oh, absolutely, and remedial English turned out to be more interesting than I had expected. Go into these organisational situations and it can happen that you find people who are able to write perfectly well to their mothers, their lovers, their spouses and the rest of it, but in their work are rendered all but illiterate. Sometimes they certainly do lack writing skills, but often their inability is connected to the fact that they have no authority to make any decisions at all. And how can you author anything without at least some measure of authority? So quite often I would be hired in to teach grammar, and would actually find myself dealing with something that was quite juicy, a problem that went to the heart of the whole organisational regime. So I spent a lot of the early 1980s travelling around the country on trains, staying in cheap hotels - a time of floral wall paper and flip charts. In spare moments I was writing about what seemed to be going on in the national culture, and that was what became my first book, *On Living in an Old Country*, which came out in 1985.

That book hit a nerve, albeit in a rather haphazard way. The peculiarity of my personal perspective as a distanced and pretty alienated returnee from Canada (it's there that Britain is referred to as 'the old country') coincided unexpectedly with the wider cultural and political trends that were activating the idea of tradition in the national context. Margaret Thatcher was a moderniser. Her project was to break through the traditions of the post-war political consensus, yet it was plain in the early 1980s that it also involved the reassertion of older continuities. I noticed, for example, that the Falklands campaign coincided with a major triumph of marine archaeology, the resurrection of Henry VIII's flagship, the Mary Rose, which was pulled up from the bottom of the Solent estuary, where it had been buried for many centuries. It was all on national television, and as that sodden hulk broke into view the excited presenter announced that this was 'the first time *we* have seen this in 437 years'. I was impressed by the parallels with the Falklands war, which happened at more or less the same time, and the celebrations that welcomed the triumphant task force home: there again it was all about how *we* had gone and recovered something that was truly ours. So I noticed coincidences of that sort: this 'we' that was being used in very different domains, and also that the agenda of conservation and restoration of monuments and that stuff, which one associates with fairly specialist, innocent, affably British and perhaps almost eccentric preoccupations, was becoming metaphorically active at the centre of the national culture. Saving the heritage was no longer a matter of propping up the falling walls of Dover Castle, say; it was much more about armouring yourself against the threat of 'the enemy within'. We have the nation, that's us, and then we have these threats. The rhetoric of 'Heritage and Danger' may once have belonged to community activists, art historians and curators, but suddenly it seemed to be all over the place. So, I noticed that going on, and that is where my first book came from.

You are not the only one who made that kind of discovery. I'm thinking of a book like The Invention of Tradition *of 1983.*

Yes, Eric Hobsbawm's (and Terence Ranger's) book; and the issue had also been broached by people like Tom Nairn, who had looked at English identity from the point of view of a Scot who hoped for a loosening of the British state. I would say that this perception of tradition came out of the left primarily. Conservatives have tended to assume tradition, to want more of it, but not to see it as this kind of problem. But even on the left, it was a thin field at that time. When I started writing on these matters, in 1980 or so, I looked around for people who had thought about it before. I remember going to the library to consult the critical literature on 'nationalism' - for it was obviously a form of nationalism I was observing. And to my amazement, I discovered that, with the exception of Gramsci (then being re-read by Stuart Hall and others), the Marxist tradition - the left intellectual tradition - hardly recognised nationalism except as a third-world development stratagem or resistance movement. The idea that it might exist in a developed European country like Britain, or come to be lined up against the progressivism of the welfare state as seemed then to be happening here, was apparently all but unthinkable.

But this has changed, hasn't it? Your project is part of a larger movement. In the last ten or fifteen years, quite a number of rather good books have been written about nationhood and constructions of nationhood, Benedict Anderson's Imagined Communities: Reflections on the Origin and Spread of Nationalism, *for instance, or Richard Holgerson's* Forms of Nationhood.

It was already emerging as a major theme. Looking back on it, my book seems to have helped create awareness of the way in which conservationist, architectural and curatorial concerns were being overshadowed by broader national issues - ghosted, if you like, by at times thoroughly morbid social polemic. People involved in museums, archaeology and similar fields found their preoccupations highly active in their metaphorical significance. Their sense of emergency, especially, was finding wider social resonance. For many years, the campaigner's tactic had been to identify a valuable 'heritage', and then denounce the 'dangers' threatening to encroach on it. Anyone who questioned this polarising rhetoric was likely to be condemned instantly as being on the side of the vandals. I have never had any argument with the campaigners who tried to stop speculative redevelopment of the sort that gutted many European cities after the Second World War, But when this idea of heritage goes into wider circulation and is used in a more diffuse way, it can become decidedly questionable; and that certainly happened in Britain in the post-war decades.

Hobsbawm and Ranger's book *The Invention of Tradition* made a very strong argument about the ways in which tradition may be synthetically created by governing regimes at any particular point in time. My own view on the 'invention' of tradition was that basically it's true, but then you must quickly move on to a second question: so what? In bad uses of this argument, you quickly get into a situation where you're behaving as if it is enough to point out that a tradition is 'invented' - as if that was a total falsification, and therefore the end of the matter. But in fact that is where questions should start not end. If traditions are synthetically created, then you have to ask why and consider how they work. You also have to recognise that there may be considerable authenticity in the way in which people experience and think about invented traditions, and that demands careful handling - certainly not just facile deconstruction.

You often chose to write about small, apparently even anecdotal events, and to build up a larger picture through them. As, for instance, the British telephone boxes that feature both in A Journey Through Ruins *and in* The Village that Died for England. *Why?*

To describe someone as an anecdotalist would, under many circumstances, be to insult them. It implies triviality, an inability to look beyond minor occurrences, and not being able to distinguish the wood from the trees. But I found myself fascinated by fragmentary events that seemed to have a certain radioactivity about them, and then started exploring and, as it were, unpacking them. Partly this suited my circumstance - I didn't have the time for concentrated work. But I also developed this method, if one can call it that, at a time when British intellectual culture, or at least the part I was involved in, was locked into the most ludicrously abstract theory. This stratospheric conjecturing got a few people into academic jobs or onto the North American conference circuit. It was also opening the way for 'post-colonial studies', but to me then it seemed more like a cloud than a lens through which to view the changes that Thatcher and others were carrying out on the ground. I'm not at all sure that it was helpful for the next generation of students, many of whom never seem to have made it through the endless reading list.

So it's true that telephone boxes do loom quite large in my books. That is partly because they were the symbol of public service that English conservatives finally felt obliged to defend in the 1980s. But there is something else about these small occasions which can then be proved to have much more general significance. They reveal that there is a role for critical elucidation, that causalities do exist, that there are deeper coherences to be found even in apparently superficial events. For me this is the best legacy of the western Marxist tradition - I'm thinking of writers like Ernst Bloch, whose book *Heritage of these Times* fascinated me in the early eighties, and Walter Benjamin too.

He also had that gift for focusing on seemingly irrelevant, meaningless details and then reading them as significant signs ...

... and of finding epic currents in apparently superficial little dramas. All my books have been written at a time when the political and intellectual framework that I come from - the left wing intellectual tradition of cultural and historical analysis - has been in considerable disrepair. It has not been advancing, and a lot of energy has gone into entrenchment and holding on to already established and sometimes wholly inadequate positions. But if you go out and look at what is actually going on around you, you can still find things out, and, more important, you can get ahead of yourself and into situations that demand more than the routine application of a threadbare interpretative framework. So it's a way of keeping things open, and certainly not of proving that absolutely everything can be explained from the same static point of view.

What you are calling your anecdotal method... do you see that as in any way related to a larger epistemological sweep over the last thirty years: the farewell and the goodbye to the 'grand recit', to the 'grand narrative'? What we have is stories rather than History, and in many stories we have details and these details can be luminous, or they can be made luminous. My metaphor of "luminous details" is taken from Ezra Pound - you never mention Ezra Pound, but he looms in the background of some of your book.

I read Pound a lot when I was in Canada, and I'm interested that you should mention him now. I haven't made any deliberate derivations there, but I got my bearings in that North American school of poetics where the poem is 'a field of meaning', and I've since learned to appreciate what the elderly Pound meant when he wrote about the difficulty of making things 'cohere'. I studied with Robin Blaser, a poet who put his own emphasis on the idea of 'territory'. And I learned a lot about the possibilities of place from the writings of Charles Olson, an American and partly 'Poundian' poet - an 'archaeologist of morning' in his own phrase - who wrote an epic series called *The Maximus Poems* about his home town of Gloucester in Massachusetts.

I'm not talking about political positions. I'm talking about the textuality of your texts which, like Pound's texts, are texts that bring details and make them luminous. Whole stories are opened up in details, and also they are texts that introduce so many characters, so many positions and so many voices. Some of the details you introduce are individual characters. What I find so impressive about your books and particularly about The Village That Died for England *is the wealth of characters.*

It's amazing what you find when you scratch the ground in the right places. I look at mainstream histories of British culture in the twentieth century and I am depressed by them. You look at what the average Oxford Professor of literature or whatever produces if he decides to write a book about the thirties, and it tends to be so predictable. The same writers are likely to feature, with one given a bit more emphasis and another thrust back towards the shadows. It's as if they are all dipping into the same filing cabinet, and then writing in order to prove that there is really nothing more to say. With a lot of this academic writing you get no sense either that the period was alive with danger and tension, or, more generally, that British culture has produced the most extreme eccentricities of attitude - and moreover that some of the most live stuff is right over there in the margins. A large part of my *The Village that Died For England* is concerned with the 1920s and 1930s, and yet there is only the slightest correlation between the writers and thinkers featured there and those who appear in Valentine Cunningham's recent book on the literary culture of the 1930s.

As for the other matter, of finding a diversity of voices and allowing details to speak, well I am all for it. Minor and accidental things can be pregnant with meaning and indication, but only if at some point you're prepared to say that you don't exactly know where you're going. In that sense I am a travel writer, albeit one who travels with the help of archives and old books rather than locomotion. But I don't actually know where I'll end up when I start these books.

They just coalesce gradually?

I work them through. When I started *The Village that Died for England* I thought I was dealing with an entirely post- Second World War story. I had noticed this moving but also banal story - an anecdote, to be sure - about this remote and insignificant place called Tyneham that kept surfacing in newspapers and radio programmes. They called it 'The village that died for D-Day', and talked about the way it had been evacuated during the war. It was a minor story of patriotic sacrifice, which was then betrayed by the post-war peace. The village was never returned to civilian use, and with it went one of the most beautiful stretches of the southern Dorset coast, the heartland of England, part of Thomas Hardy's Wessex. Now, to begin with I thought this story began in the Second World War, because it was about the village that was evacuated. And I wanted to write about it as a kind of fable that dramatised energies and problems in the post-war period. But of course as I started digging, I realised that I was into something more like an English Pompeii, and that I had to go much further back. I didn't know what I was going to find. I had no idea I was going to come across Rolf Gardiner, for example, the father of the conductor John Eliot Gardiner, and his extraordinary connections with the *Wandervogel* movement and the *Deutsche Freischar*, with, as it turned out, some more disastrous aspects of the German 1920s and early 1930s.

What you unfold is a whole spectrum of political positions - fascism and communism, the orthodox Stalinist Communism of Sylvia Townsend Warner, the poet...

... entirely, mixed with Bloomsbury high-mindedness...

... and then you get a number of esoteric, anarchist and ecological groups. Indeed, the book works towards presenting England or Britain in epitome or microcosm. What

you present is a model for something greater than the sacrifice of a village. I think that it is the 'pars pro toto' form of representation that holds your books together, that all your books share.

I decided early on that I wanted to write about Britain, and I wanted to write in the present. I didn't want to adopt an entirely literary voice because, although I come from and am informed by literary studies (I mean I'm more that than I'm a sociologist or historian) I couldn't make any of the available genres work for me. I wanted a contemporary prose that could be descriptive, analytical, dramatic as well as more personal, and sometimes more journalistic too. I could have tried to write fiction, and I could have tried to become a straight-down-the-line literary historian, but the subject matter I was after didn't make that kind of sense.

The question of unity was certainly also an issue. One of the problems of working within a geographical framework is that you're often standing in something like a field full of rabbits, which are endlessly darting into different holes in the ground. You could be following them in a hundred different directions for ever. But I still prefer to be somewhat disorganised around a chosen place than to try squeezing everything into a simplistic chronological unity that imposes an external shape. I wanted a much more open form, and that was the point at which I decided to opt for territory over genre. Mind you, I don't think this is the same as writing purely local history. Publishers and booksellers may sometimes end up filing these books under 'local history', but I think that's quite wrong, partly because that idea of the 'local' implies its own diminishment of place. Anyway, as I said earlier, I think a territory is very different from a place on a map. It's got more dimensions, its not all resolved, and it doesn't disclose itself along a single perspective. It's an argument as well as a locality, and if you work it through properly, you'll find it's a microcosm too, just as you say.

There's actually a time-honoured term for that, for the description of places, and that is 'chorography'. It is a well-established genre of describing a certain territory in the Renaissance. Still, you do it differently from the chorographers of the Early Modern period, who tried systematically to enumerate all the facts and assets of a place: you focus on one rather small territory, say Dalston Lane in London, or

Tyneham in Dorset, as small-scale models for the modern British city or the English countryside, and then, still within that territory, you again focus on particular aspects.

That's right, and I've had some interesting arguments about this over the years. Raphael Samuel, the late people's historian, used to be rather wary of my approach, which I think he thought violated the participatory ethics of local testimony. He remarked, for example, that it was odd to write about Dalston without paying due respect to the richness of local dialects, Cockney or otherwise. I'm not opposed to that kind of testimony, even if it can rapidly become sentimental, but rather than just trying to document the human flora and fauna of a chosen territory, I wanted to use that territory as a yardstick, a kind of analytical device. So I chose a place that is not just small but, in its social and cultural content, also as intensified as possible, where sharp differences exist, which is full of history and yet free from any uniform design - including one that might be imposed in the name of 'heritage'. And then I used it as a prism through which to trace wider stories.

And how do you find your territories?

With *A Journey through Ruins*, it was a matter of waking up to where I was already. I used to walk down Dalston Lane twice, three, four, five times a day, and yet I had never really noticed it, except I suppose in accordance with the usual welfare state perspective of deprivation etc. And then I looked and realised, well, here we are in this absolutely modest and ordinary stretch of East London, with its rotting Victorian buildings, its hard-pressed shop keepers, its chaotic bus-stops, its hobbling public library and its famously corrupt police station; and this huge transformation called Thatcherism is taking place, shaking things out of their customary affiliations. Being unusually dishevelled, Dalston Lane was partly like a posthumous relic of the world gone by. But it was also like a history book: you could see fifty years of failed social idealism in its charity shops alone. And, of course, thanks to the political changes of that time, it was also undergoing what looked like terminal shock treatment. Everything seemed slightly disconnected, and slightly raw. Then I discovered that the street had been scheduled for demolition for almost the entire length of the post-war period, and its unlikely survival gave it extra resonance in the year or two after Margaret Thatcher had been deposed by her own Conservative Party.

This also led me to thinking more generally about the place of the inner city in the wider British imagination. To read a certain kind of British social commentary, which can be found in a liberal paper like the *Guardian* as well as in tabloids like the *Sun*, you would think the inner city was a place where people got mugged and raped and robbed, and where 'multiculturalism' was a major disaster. In reality, terrible things do happen in East London and other inner city areas. Yet despite their problems these areas are, for most of the time, stable and even quite industrious places where people spend an awful lot of time not raping and mugging and robbing each other. So I wanted to use Dalston to measure the distance between the reality of the place and this constant rhetoric of onlooking judgement. I wanted to use it to trace the story of post-war social policy. I also wanted to get into the mix of the city a bit, and to give at least some expression to that characteristic inner city style of perception, where one person's take on the place is never the same as anyone else's. I like that aspect of city life very much: that if you're a sympathetic city dweller, you know that the way you see and use the city is only ever one part of the story. It's like common rights applied to the urban street: we walk and interpret and use the place, in the full knowledge that people with other backgrounds are at the same time doing it very differently. That urban outlook is quite different from the rural way of thinking about place, which, at least in its traditional cultural expression, is all about continuity and deep settlement, single vision and organic placidity.

So Dalston seemed to assemble itself in my mind as I wrote that book, and I decided, well OK, I'm just going to stick with this small stretch of street, and I'm going to use it as a measuring stick for the things that seem to be happening around here. I used to research on my feet, often in the company of Iain Sinclair, the poet and novelist, who has been digging into that patch for many years now. If I'd written it conventionally it would have been a study of fifty years of enlightened social policy, starting with the relief schemes developed during the blitz, which set the precedent for the later welfare state. I was writing the book in the fiftieth anniversary of the Blitz, when so many elderly East Enders were getting out into the parks, and they were flying Lancasters and Spitfires overhead to commemorate the RAF, and also campaigning for statues to Bomber Harris - the man who blew out the lungs of all those people in Dresden. There was something desperate about this delayed commemoration, with its insistence on a war memory that nobody had thought to mark with statues in the years immediately after the war. So I was seeing the end of that memory, and thinking about what had happened to the Welfare State that came out of the Blitz.

So the book does not just tell stories; the stories do add up to something, and I think that would also apply to The Village that Died for England. *One way of putting what they add up to is a sort of apocalyptic vision, which I find to a certain extent disturbing. The subtitle of* A Journey Through Ruins *is already apocalyptic - The Last Days of London. The tanks in* The Village that Died for England *are in themselves an apocalyptic image: they might come straight from the Book of Revelation, actually.*

And indeed, for the inventors and first observers of those machines, they did.

The Village that Died for England: *again death, 'things coming to an end', a Yeatsian phrase which you take up occasionally. What does that apocalypse consist of? Is it the end of the Welfare State? Is it...*

That's a very good question. When I was writing A Journey Through Ruins and gave it the subtitle *The Last Days of London*, the publishers were so depressed that in the end I was persuaded to put another, rather stupid subtitle into the third edition. But in truth it was and is *The Last Days of London*. Partly that title came from my observation that in the late 1980s there was a considerable interest in debris in the avant garde galleries, a sort of postmodernist celebration of ruin, garbage, junk. Even the imagery of the old slum interior that reformers had worked so hard to abolish twenty years earlier, was being rehabilitated and presented as if it was a kind of ready-made art installation. So partly, when I talked about the last days of London, I was referring to this sort of morbidity, to what happens to an avant garde culture when it loses its social or political base. And the answer is that it gets onto the rubbish tip. I called this the aesthetics of the second blitz, a romanticisation of the ruins of the welfare state.

At the same time, I allowed that phrase to stand as a subtitle because there is a more serious sense of finality in the book. A few people said, this is far too negative, of course London isn't ending. And that is true in one sense, although in another and as you must know, coming from Berlin, death and rebirth are part of the fabric of every city's life. And what was in its last days in the London I was writing about was the post-war settlement, the idea of planned reform that had emerged after the Second World War. That whole idea of the city that was to be rebuilt by the enabling state was dying, both from the failure of its own works, and from the attack unleashed by Margaret Thatcher - an attack that included the sacking of the Greater London Council. The whole structure of that civic understanding was being taken to pieces, and hideous ghosts were surfacing from a suppressed Dickensian past. I remember using one episode in particular. A body was found floating in a shallow ornamental pond in one of Hackney's public parks, and there was this terrible account in the *Hackney Gazette* of how it had been there for weeks. Kids had been fishing and sailing their model boats around it, and the police and park officials had shared the same illusion: namely that it was just a black garbage bag. Hackney's refuse collection service was in its usual abysmal state, and everyone had assumed that this drowned man was just another abandoned bag of rubbish. So that is what 'the end' was about, and I certainly wasn't intending to celebrate it.

Meanwhile, the whole political culture, and certainly the whole public sector, was becoming increasingly dominated by a curious managerial realism, of which we have certainly not yet seen the end. Where once there used to be a sense of cause and effect, people started to talk endlessly about 'change', about 'managing change', as if they were surfers on a wave for which no one could expect them to take any responsibility. Euphemisms like 'creating underspend' started to be used in place of more honest phrases like 'cuts'. This sort of managerial language now covers vast areas of urban administration and policy. If you look at what stands for policy in the Labour Party nowadays, it is exactly that sort of idea. The old levers of state power have been sold off or miniaturised over the years of Conservative government, and what stands in their place is often only this weirdly detached rhetoric of efficiency. All the public policy think tanks, and all the people with an eye on the main chance as it is likely to be under Tony Blair seem to be operating with this language. So it looks to me as if the moral and political centre of post-war public administration has disintegrated too. Now there was enough wrong with those ideas to prevent one falling into simple lamentation at their passing. But there is still this gaping hole in the political culture, which no amount of marketing talk can hide. So I suppose that an apocalyptic tone was part of the business of mapping the loss of those anchors.

But don't you find yourself with strange bedfellows in that sort of construction of post-war English history? Say, with Prince Charles or with Roger Scruton?

I don't regard them as bedfellows at all. I did write at some length about Prince Charles, but then it seemed to me that that he had an interesting moment in the 1980s, before the Royal soap opera turned into a drama of marital infidelity, and when the Labour Party was so demoralised that it offered no effective opposition at all. Thatcher was shaking the country to pieces, and Prince Charles, who is constitutionally excluded from addressing mainstream political issues, was poking about in the margins picking up apparently peripheral issues on which he could legitimately take a view: the paranormal, environmentalism, the inner city, architecture etc. There is a fair measure of eccentricity in Charles, and plenty to suggest that his outlook is close to that of the old Tories, who defended an idea of ancient English hierarchy against the transformations of the free market. But it was still the case that many of the themes he picked up in the 1980s turned out to be politically far more active than he or his advisers could have expected. So suddenly there was Prince Charles, talking about public housing and civil liberties - admittedly only in Romania - and taking the side of the urban poor. I was interested in that, but I never saw it as an answer to anything and I would never have joined the camp.

No, I don't see myself as sharing common ground with either Prince Charles or Roger Scruton. Both of them seem to lament the passing of a particular version of English identity - more English than British. I'm interested in tracing out that particular mode of thought. But I don't subscribe to it. I reserve the right to be moved by the sight of an ancient English landscape or barn, but if you put me down in Tyneham village as it was before it was destroyed, I would be itching to escape. What Scruton and perhaps also Prince Charles regret is the loss of a time-sanctioned social hierarchy and the untidiness of mass democracy. I am against the sort of blithe history-less perception that is simply embarrassed by where we come from, but I'm not on the side of these Conservative lamenters. I try to reveal the emotional basis and power of this nostalgic outlook, but I also try, particularly in *The Village That Died for England*, to show the pathological consequences of defining England in purely insular and perhaps also thoroughbred terms.

Do you see yourself with this project as being in the tradition of British travel writing? Let us take Cobbett's Rural Rides, *for instance, and your books. There are, of course, enormous differences, but there are similarities as well. Cobbett has got one big theme, and that is the destruction of agriculture and rural life and culture through enclosures, 'tax-eaters,' tithes and the cancerous growth of London, the 'all-devouring Wen'. You also have one big theme. It is the ambiguities, ambivalences, ironies of the relationship between modernisation and heritage. But there is once crucial difference: Cobbett knows exactly what should be done, whereas with you one wonders, and doesn't know exactly what your position is. In* The Village that Died for England, *I have the impression that you are celebrating the wonderful weirdness and richness of the discourses about Tyneham: fascist, Stalinist, esoteric, ecological and so on. But if in the end one asks oneself, what would you actually like to see done about Tyneham, there is no answer. When it comes to Dalston Lane in London, there is again a wealth, a rich mine of insights and so on. If one asks oneself, what does he want to be done, one only gets suggestions, a recurrent one of them being that state intervention should be more effective ...*

Possibly... Let's take this in stages, because there are several things here. On Cobbett and travel: in some senses I would describe myself as an anti-travel writer. My sense is that travel writing has been full of spurious exoticism in recent years. Publishers pour out countless travel books by people who were raised in perfectly reasonable middle class houses in various parts in England, but who feel obliged to fly off to the Andes or the darkest jungle somewhere. Nowhere is safe from the British travel-writer. We've had all the possible encounters: the traveller might meet a hostile pygmy or a bear and perhaps have an amorous encounter or two. This is really an ironic, or perhaps just farcical, restaging of old colonial attitudes, although unencumbered by any version of the old white man's burden. The key question in many of these books seems to be how far you have to go before your more or less conventional British attitudes start to seem interesting. There are exceptions of course, from Robert

Byron in the 1930s, to Chatwin's *In Patagonia*, and some Colin Thubron too. But to judge by some of these books, the whole wide world has become a laboratory for testing out minor British attitudes. What I wanted to do was to see what happens if you turn that convention upside down and venture into your own landscape, with an eye to thick rather than thin description. Of course, I knew that there is a contrary tradition of that too.

This is what our book is about: the tradition that stretches, let's say, from John Leland and William Camden in the sixteenth century to Defoe and Dr. Johnson in the eighteenth century, Cobbett in the nineteenth century and Priestley and Orwell in ours - a great tradition, I would say!

It is a great tradition, and I see that. When I was working on my first book, *On Living in an Old Country*, I came across all these forgotten inter-war books about the English countryside, published by companies like Batsford - books about the old green roads of England in which people walked away from the cities and also from their memories of the 1914-18 war, and followed ancient tracks up onto the limestone, or the chalk Downs which had such unique and consoling qualities for many of these early twentieth century hunters of rural virtue. These books are often full of a passionate urgency about the places they describe, but they are valueless now, unwanted and scarcely even worth the time it would take a second hand book dealer to catalogue them. I came across a volume or series called 'The Highways and Byways of England', and it was then that I thought of trying to revive this almost entirely defunct genre for my own purposes. I had no desire to be too assertive or explicit about this. But that was where I got this idea of working with small stretches of minor road. Those pre-war writers would dwell on rural landscape, folk traditions, rural crafts, local building materials and probably flowers and butterflies too. I was more interested in matters like social conflict, memory and utopian aspiration. But it wasn't just a post-modern spoof. I like the idea of that kind of close observation. I do use my English lanes as ways of addressing wider matters, but I think there is still a kind of patriotic edge to it. I suspect I'm more in the tradition of moral outrage than of placid bird-watching pleasantries.

Indeed, the tradition of William Cobbett! In contrast to him, however, your books are not travel books because there is hardly any locomotion in them, to start with, and you, as a traveller, are almost invisible in them. Instead of dramatising yourself - as has happened so often in older travelogues and even more so in contemporary travel writing - you try to fade yourself out; you do make only very occasional appearances, where you speak about yourself, your own attitudes. I mean, you are there everywhere, but you are hardly ever present as a person in the foreground, who comments upon things.

I think there is a huge difference between what I do and the activities of some of these more light-footed and, let it be said, incomparably more successful writers like Paul Theroux [in *The Kingdom by the Sea*, 1983] or Bill Bryson [in *Notes from a Small Island*, 1995]. They pass through, rarely bothering to look twice, just taking a note of the appearances as they go. Both Bryson and Theroux took a quick glance at the gunnery range that I wrote about in *The Village that Died for England*, and Theroux didn't even stay long enough to discover that his walk was disturbed by tanks rather than artillery, as he assumed. But then for him the first impression is the whole point, and it hardly matters if it's right or wrong.

As I say, I think the difference is between thick and thin description. To begin with, I don't expect my localities to reveal much until I have been there many times over a number of years. I made repeated visits to the territory of *The Village that Died For England* - starting in the spring of 1984, when I went down there to look for the landscape that haunts Mary Butts' novels. So I have seen the place change over ten years, and watched many people come and go too. I'm not interested in the one-dimensional map. I like to see the movement of history and of power in a place before I start guessing at the dimensions of it. And what happened to me in Dorset was that, in a period when everything is being made very similar in the name of 'heritage' - same marketing devices, same logos, same roadsigns, same sort of idea of how you display and exploit history - I found a genuinely historical twentieth century landscape that, for obvious and explosive reasons, had escaped this simplistic sort of exposition. It was a place one could really think about the century with, and if I still like the book it is because I reckon that on that very localised firing range, I found a story that is uniquely telling about modern English culture.

Similarly, with Dalston Junction and the urban territory of *A Journey Through Ruins*: I had lived in that part of London for fifteen years. I do my fair share of walking about and going from one place to another, but I think probably I see my role much more as a sifter and as the person who tries to lay things bare, and to dramatise the meanings in a place. Cobbett, as you say, was doing something quite different. To begin with, he knows what he thinks. He is there with a clearly defined social and political outlook doing the business, gathering evidence. I don't feel that I have the answers to the problems that come up, and I don't see it as my role to tell people what to think. If I make autobiographical appearances in these books, it is partly in order to establish that they aren't written from an omniscient or universal perspective. And anyway, in this time of dissolved political certainties, it is at least better than nothing to keep questions, complexities and also potentialities open.... In the meantime, so to speak....This is meantime writing.

So the local history shelf would be the wrong shelf for the these books?

I think so. I'm not a localist, even though I use localities to articulate what I take to be bigger themes. But the books do end up on the local history shelf, which can be very frustrating. *A Journey Through Ruins* got coded as an east London book, and *The Village that Died for England* sometimes turns up alongside bucolic 'country living' books, although I think having any reference to 'death' in your title makes for some awkwardnesses there.

Well that's the consequence of falling between genres, isn't it.

Yes, but where else is there to be? These books couldn't exist without falling between genres - a problem for marketing people, but not for the people who do actually seek them out and read them. *The Village that Died for England* may well be locally situated, in that contested landscape where two versions of the English pastoral - the downland being one and, as I argue, the tank being another - have been in collision for seventy years. But what kept me digging away down there was precisely its wider ramifications. We all know, for example, that environmentalism is good. But nobody ever seems to map the history of the green or conservationist impulse. It's always expressed in terms of immediate necessity, an immediate appeal to the good. And yet on this patch of Dorset, which campaigners have been trying to 'save' from the military for the best part of seventy years, one could see its history - that it has had very different and at times contradictory expressions, some positively alarming. That was one of the wider stories I was after. And as I proceeded, I found that this small area of Dorset was indeed a genuine microcosm, and that the tension between the tanks and the landscape took a different but always telling shape in every decade. So the book became a kind of narrative history of twentieth century English utopianism, and a seriously bizarre story it turned out to be. Strange, for example, to find the army, which for decades has been opposed as the despoiler of this landscape, now playing the green card itself, and claiming to have conserved this landscape from even more inappropriate use. These days, even the shell craters are described as habitats for rare downland plants.

And what makes it so bizarre is the range of idealisms and utopias from the extreme left to the extreme right.

Yes, there too I think the story is broadly allegorical. We do seem to live in a century where the edges of the spectrum curl up and meet. If you go to the left now in British political culture, you will find ideas that, five years previously you would have found on the anti-statist right. This cross-over is part of what is being captured or revealed in these books, and it is especially pronounced when it comes to ecological themes. Somebody once told me that I liked to confuse the jump leads, but I think its history that's done that, not me.

Let's take the Gardiner family as an example!

An interesting case, to be sure, and all expressed on a stretch of land that runs along the edge of Cranborne Chase, a chalk plateau in North Dorset. The land is presently farmed organically by John Eliot Gardiner, who is also a major international conductor, known not just as a driving force in the authentic instruments movement and the founder and director of the Monteverdi Choir, but for his strong use of rhythm, particularly in early polyphonic music. My researches were concerned with the generation before that, and with John Eliot's father, Rolf Gardiner, who campaigned for Tyneham in the 1960s. He was against the military occupation of that land, which he saw as the culmination of the modern state's extinction of the organic rural way of life. He also opposed a nuclear installation that was built nearby with all the usual, soon to be broken, promises and reassurances. Once the army were removed, he had plans to turn the Tyneham area into a pilot project for the symbolic restoration of an England that he saw as all but extinguished by modern developments, from cars and roads, to centralised state policy, to international finance. Gardiner was an interesting, and in many ways prescient, environmental thinker - a European, rather than just a bunkered little Englander. He pioneered ecological initiatives on his family estates in Malawi, and he was involved in the formation of an early international committee to promote the idea of 'landscape husbandry' in Europe. There is a lot of currency in his arguments about the countryside and its future now that its traditional forms, in which he saw beauty and utility combined, have become agriculturally redundant. And yet this was a man who, twenty years after his death, was still being denounced as a grisly, patriarchal fascist. If he appears in books, it tends to be in claimed association with the *Frei Korps,* and the local memory is pretty rich too. I found that some people who lived near his home in North Dorset remembered all sorts of elaborate folk dancing and ritual and muttered about him as 'that Nazi'.

Clearly, this was an interesting figure, and all the more so, as I say, since Rolf Gardiner was an early ecological thinker - attuned to those themes long before the late 1960s, when he made somewhat eccentric utterances about the dawn of the Post-Modern Age. So I started looking into his background, and discovered that Rolf Gardiner had grown up in Berlin before the First World War. His father Alan Gardiner was an Egyptologist, who was in Germany to work on the dictionary of hieroglyphics. So Gardiner, whose family was decidedly well off, was raised in Berlin and came back to England shortly before the First World War. As that war raged he was at school - first Rugby and then the famously 'progressive' and coeducational institution called Bedales - and then he went up to Cambridge, where we find him immediately after the war, reading D.H. Lawrence, remembering Germany, and trying to keep the two halves of his Anglo-German experience together. In the early 1920s he came up with his own programme of war reparations. An ardent believer in the idea of 'youth', he pledged his loyalty to his own 'generation' - an idea that was very prominent after the First World War - and started visiting Germany in the vacations. He went on vast walking tours, organised a temporary theatre company and toured Shakespeare, in an attempt to remind German youth of matters more profound than polarised national hatreds, and he took folk dancing troups too. By 1923, Gardiner had become much involved with the Bund, with the German youth movements, and, a little later, he took part in the early work-camps pioneered at youth centres - including those run in Silesia in the late 1920s by Professor Rosenstock-Huessy, who would flee Germany as soon as Hitler came to power.

As you know better than I, this whole movement, if we can call it this, was overtaken, incorporated and extinguished by Nazism; and Gardiner, who had started out fairly close to thinkers like Ruskin and William Morris, with the naive idea of applying something like Guild Socialism across Northern Europe, started making all sorts of deplorable utterances, even as he disapproved of Nazi excesses. I wasn't interested in diminishing the extent to which he may have been a fellow traveller, but where others have been content simply to denounce him as a Nazi, I wanted to trace out how an English rural revivalist, a folk dancing advocate of 'rhythm' and organic farming who used early polyphonic song as a metaphor for political and ecological harmony, ended up on the fascist road. All this was particularly interesting, since Gardiner was without doubt a genuinely ecological thinker. And he was also remarkably uncontrite about many of his friendships in Germany - he was still writing to Hitler's agricultural minister, Walter Darré, after the Second World War, and he persisted in anti-Semitic remarks too - as, no doubt, did many members of his pre-war circle, who believed that 'usury' was responsible for the troubles of native English agriculture. As for John Eliot Gardiner, I was a little nervous of approaching him, but he was very helpful. He had fought his own battles with his father - and not just about his decision to perform music within the professional domain that his father, who thought music should be connected to the soil and performed within the agricultural setting, disdained as the 'discarnate' bourgeois concert hall. John Eliot may farm organically on many of the same acres, and his ideas on polyphony and rhythm may in some way still be connected to the musical outlook of his father, but he long ago took his distance from the dodgy organicism of his father's political vision.

Let us go back to the question of prescription ...

I am indeed interested in opening up all these cultural backgrounds, even many that are dismissed as eccentric and peripheral by more mainstream historians. I do so in the belief that these histories may still inform the present, or at least indicate the dangers of certain purist positions, including the ecological one. But having done that, why should I tie it all up into a neat conclusion? I don't think prescriptive certainties are particularly useful in this sort of enquiry. I'm not writing a cookbook, after all, or seeking to replace history with recipes for the future. My role is, rather, to identify the sheer range of polarisation and of difference which has existed within English self-understanding, and to show how it has functioned to inspire and also to limit thought at any particular time. Looking at this 1930s ecologism, for example, it is no wonder either that a lot of people had their doubts about greenery, when it resurfaced in the 1960s, or that environmental campaigns are inclined to bitter internal disputation.

If you ask me to summarise my main concerns I would say that I'm interested in the extent to which, over the fifty years since the Second World War, we have seen a polarisation between ideas of traditional English identity, symbolised by ancient country houses, the rural landscape etc., and contrary ideas of state-led modernisation gone wrong. In *A Journey Through Ruins* my central image for the latter are the tower blocks, images of alienation which are among the primary architectural symbols of the post-war period. Brideshead versus the towerblocks - that was one of the leading oppositions of the period, and it pitched the traditional time-sanctioned nation against an image of destructive modernisation gone wrong. To point this out is not to say that many other things weren't going on, but that particular polarisation became a primary political metaphor by the 1980s, and it certainly determined the way we in this country said farewell to the welfare state. Of course, it was grossly oversimplified and it imposed a brutal closure on public thought.

So your method is that of a dramatist? You actually speak about dramatising meanings and, like a dramatist, you refrain from inculcating a certain interpretation, and allow your readers to draw their own conclusions from the materials you present.

I guess mine is more of a literary method than a theorist's one - at least in the sense that I think readers should be left to make what they will of the results. I'm not pretending to be neutral or omniscient. I'll certainly take positions and make judgements as I go along, but I don't see why a writer should be expected to resolve things that, in actuality, plainly remain unresolved. Chris Cutler, a musician with a zealous left-wing past, once told me that having a fairly simplified political outlook could be vital in your youth - the only thing that enables you to think with any measure of independence, especially at a time when values are so relativised. I reckon that may well be true, but I've had enough of paying dues according to crudely drawn party lines. When you are trying to get the measure of cultural realities, the rush to judgement just gets in the way.

You are non-judgemental. I mean, you don't denigrate your characters, you always try to be fair to them and allow them to put forward their own point of view.

And I also have to ask questions of myself. Do I know, for example, can I be absolutely certain that, had I been living at that particular time, say the 1930s, when a certain sort of anti-Semitic attitude was actually quite widely distributed through British society, that I would have remained absolutely innocent of it? I profoundly hope that I would have done, but those attitudes were certainly still around when I was at school in Dorset in the 1960s, and I don't think any of us can be entirely sure. This makes the idea of merely denying, or denouncing toxic attitudes in the past seem a little bit too quick to me. The same can be said about poets like Ezra Pound and T.S. Eliot. It may seem remarkable that Eliot, say, was content to republish some of his more anti-Semitic pre-war lines after the Holocaust, and without any real attempt at explanation. Yet, at the same time, these attitudes do not make him a worthless poet. We have to allow for this range of complexities, if we are going to understand how ideas work in history. The same can be said for ecology, which, as I discovered, was incubated in a pretty foul cradle here in Britain. I'm all for 'ecological comity', but the folkish kind of eugenic organicism espoused by the 1930s ecologists who coined that phrase is repulsive. With ecology, these are not just historical problems either. We should always be watchful when politics becomes biopolitics, when it disappears into the body or into nature - because if you're not careful you end up trading in essences and short-circuiting the whole process of reason and accountability. It may once have been possible to understand Nature as the ground of being and society, but as Marilyn Strathern has pointed out, something strange has happened by the time saving wild habitats has come to be all mixed up with not eating harmful additives in food. I think we need to keep an eye on this confusion of culture and nature, and not rush to turn it into a new ecological priniciple.

Will you continue to watch that? Or, to put it more bluntly, what are your further projects? You have dealt with the country in The Village that Died for England. *You have dealt with the city in* A Journey Through Ruins ...

I sometimes feel that I'm through with writing about Britain in this concentrated way. I've written two books which are, in a sense, my autobiography. They are about the world I grew up in - that rather uniform world of post-war austerity, which was both virtuous and somewhat rationed in attitude, and which I remember as a child. So I wanted to catch all that - the fate of its reforming state, and meaning of its much loved rural landscape.... But I've done that now, and I'm not hunting for another English 'territory' to dig into. One of the reasons I wrote about England, especially in its rural dimension, was in order to think about and perhaps also expose some of the forms and consequences of our famous 'insularity'. But I don't want to press on to the point where I become a representative of that tradition!

The world outside England is, however, not very present in your books.

No it's not.

It's quite amazing, you know: Europe - in the sense of the Continent - plays a very minor role; apart from this English/German fascist connection it rarely provides a context or background. Equally minor is the role the old Commonwealth plays.

That's right, up to a point. It is there when I can find it in the record. I was pleased, let me tell you, when I finally found someone of Afro-Caribbean extraction walking into the Tyneham valley in the early seventies. But Tyneham, particularly, has served as the Europhobe's heartland - part of its symbolic potency was that it could be mythologised as the England that never experienced immigration or the reforming welfare state, and which never got dragged into the European Community. In exposing that, I was trying to show the levels of eccentricity that follow when the English turn in on themselves and try to refound their world on what is left of their rural roots. So I think this context you mention is implicit in the whole approach, rather than merely absent. And I think it true to say that neither book has provided much consolation for those who would like to think of themselves as English thoroughbreds.

I gave A Journey Through Ruins *to one of my students who wrote an essay on non-fictional accounts of multiculturalism in Britain. And she read through it and came back and said, there is very little of it in your book. At first, I wouldn't believe it, but going through the whole book again, I had to agree with her.*

That is true, but once again, only up to a point. There is a lot in that book about the response to immigration: the revaluation of tradition against it, the fable of the disappearing immigrant in the gentrifying area of Spitalfields, the wider demonisation of the inner city which is often precisely to do with fears of hybridity and 'degeneration'. These themes are all there in the book. But it is quite true that I did not go into that part of east London saying 'where is the multi-cultural reality and can I appoint myself its recorder, or its oral historian.' This would have seemed presumptuous, since the whole point of multiculturalism is about diversity and a multiplicity of viewpoints, which must be allowed to speak for themselves.

But it is also true to say that I had another priority in writing *A Journey Through Ruins*. I was concerned with tracing out what had happened to particular ideas of administration and planning - a perspective that was sharpened by the experience I had during the 1980s. For five years I was responsible for running a small unit for the National Council for Voluntary Organisations. We were concerned with devising forms of management for voluntary and community organisations, so I spent quite a lot of time working close to organisations connected to a great many different sections of the urban population, and trying to get things done within a changing social policy framework. So the core of that book is concerned with social policy, privatisation and changing perceptions of the welfare state. This all bears heavily on the shape and possibilities of the multicultural city, as does the managerialism that increasingly seems to stand in for public policy. I'm inclined to insist on this wider political history when I meet advocates of post-modernist 'hybridity', especially those who have long since given up thinking about the state and related matters.

Well let's go back to my last question. What will you turn to, after having turned away from England, its fantasies and utopias?

I hope these books help to blow Little England at the seams and reveal it to be full of toxins as well as balms - something quite other than the sedate, quiet, tranquil, self-contained place of customary description. But I'm not going to do that again. The book I'm writing at the moment is not focused only on Britain, although it has its origins in the Dorset book. It's about the machine I found on that organic landscape - the tank, a gruesome British invention first used during the Great War. To begin with I saw this infernal engine only as a despoiler of the landscape, but I soon realised that it has a compulsive imaginative attraction for many people, and, moreover, that this was one of the reasons why the Ministry of Defence has been able to hold onto that corner of Dorset despite generations of protestation. A fair number of people preferred tanks to aristocratic pastoralism. So I started looking at this machine, and I discovered that it too was an embodiment of English culture, a product in some ways of the literary imagination. H. G. Wells foresaw tanks, and his short-story 'The Land Iron Clads', published a decade before the Great War broke out, was read by the first engineers. The first tactician, whose thinking influenced Hitler's generals as they devised the Blitzkrieg, was a follower of the occultist and charlatan Aleister Crowley, and the first expounder of his deliberately 'transgressive' poetic. And then I realised that this machine, which started off as a sort of cultural phantom, which was then crudely materialised for military use, still works as a cultural phantom - and that this is part of its effectiveness as a weapon. Whether it's Boris Yeltsin standing on one outside the White House, or that famous episode in Tiananmen Square, the tank has become a global icon of state power, history, irreversible force. And so I am trying to deal with this. I want to track this story down, and see how this machine has operated as one of the primary symbols of the twentieth century.

A history of tanks, or of fantasies about tanks ...

It's about the fantasy of tanks, but I hope to show how that fantasy has become part of the tank's practical force as a weapon. I will not be writing a book of machine worship of the kind that is often written about weapons - that really would be tank pornography. I've been travelling a bit for this book, as you can imagine - to the USA, Turkey, and into the former Soviet bloc: Poland, Slovakia and other places where people have these machines rolling around in the back of their minds - a different collection for each generation. Under Stalin, the tank became symbolic of the cutting edge of history - it was like the vanguard of that awful idea of progress, so I'm after that as well.

One might also think of the Berlin Uprising or the Prague Spring. Indeed many of the symbolic moments of 20th century history have been provided with an exclamation mark by this Beast of Revelation.

It was probably the people of East Europe who defined our perception of the tank in the 1950s and 1960s. They were the people who produced the image of this machine as seen from the street by the subjected citizen, whose state has gone to war on its own people. There's a lot to be said about mechanisation as a pre-war philosophy, and also about the moveable nature of the associated 'tank doctrine'. Ideas that were first developed by British tank theorists, and such people do exist, are then developed in Nazi Germany, and after that in Israel. So this idea of concentrated force and mobility, which again is a cultural idea at root, is turned into a moveable doctrine as it passes from one national setting to another through the century. I'm looking into the more recent idea of 'digitisation' too, with the tank reconfigured around the virtual battlefield. 'Digitisation' is very similar to mechanisation as an outlook, and I've been in Kentucky to find out about it. I spent some time at the US Armor Centre at Fort Knox - a place of tanks, gold and country and western songs. I managed to get a five day tour, a surprisingly high level one, with many of the soldiers who ran Desert Storm. They had me driving an Abrams M1A1 through a nameless German town, in simulation of course. And I'm still sorting my way through all these tapes of tank soldiers talking about the future. Enough to say that the fantasy persists. These soldiers are weirdly philosophical: tank-

Hegelians, who talk about 'The Army After Next', and have long since dissolved the tank back into its 'concept', in order to ensure that this heavy, lumbering machine will find a place in the twenty-first century. So at the end of the century, the tank is being dissolved back into its idea - a phantom again, just as it was at the beginning.

So you are abandoning the territorial approach. But what you will retain is to write about fantasies, utopias, nightmares, anxieties and their political power.

Yes absolutely, and traditions too. And there is another word for what all this is about. I was talking recently with Robin Blaser, the poet I studied with in Canada, and who visited Britain last year. We stood outside the BBC's Broadcasting House, with its relief sculptures by Eric Gill, and talked about the passing of this idea of the one truth that this now rather quaint looking building promised to beam, with parental care, over the entire world. He is, I think, rather more at ease with the postmodernist agenda than I am. Flawed as they certainly were, I still somewhat regret the loosening of the supposedly enlightened ideas of public reason and administration, and I can't look back on the decades of the welfare state in which I grew up, albeit rather bored and none too needy, without feeling that too much of that has been abandoned. But Robin Blaser, who is gay, knows very well what that single, normative idea of the world meant for people who didn't fit into it. His view seemed to be, 'Thank God we no longer have one narrative, because it was a bad one for a lot of people', which I am sure is true. But he also described himself as an 'exodist', meaning that to write as he does nowadays is to be perpetually coming out of no longer adequate formations - intellectual, poetic, social, political. The job of the exodist is not simply to obliterate or, in avant-garde terms, to transgress as he leaves or to step out in blithe and regardless ignorance, but rather to work his way through, to sift and record and, indeed, to pay due tributes on the way. I thought that was a wonderful description of the writer's role in the late twentieth century, and I hope that I have been able to do a little of that in my books about England. I am, I suppose, an obituarist. I deal with posthumous England. Perhaps I'm melancholic, and it's a matter of disposition. But I prefer to think that it has been a job that needed doing.

History has become this huge accumulation of debris, much of it strangely disconnected, and we have to work our way through it. That does mean writing obituaries, as part of the business of defining future possibilities.

Well, having at last found the genre in which you write - the obituary - I think we can stop here. Thank you very much for your time, patience, and commitment.

Netanyahu's Oslo: peace in the slow lane

John Strawson

John Strawson *looks at the prospects for the Palestinian state.*

In November 1997, two years after the assassination of prime minister Yitzhak Rabin by a right-wing Jew, posters appeared in Jerusalem depicting the current prime minister Benjamin ('Bibi') Netanyahu wearing the keyfir scarf, so loved by Yasser Arafat. The message was clear - Benjamin Netanyahu had joined Yitzhak Rabin as a traitor in the eyes a section of the Israeli right. Netanyahu's crime was to be planning to withdraw from another small tract of land in the occupied West Bank in line with Oslo peace accords with the Palestinians. While Netanyahu had been elected prime minister with the support of the right in May 1996 he had not been elected on a specifically anti-Oslo ticket. While he was no Rabin, Netanyahu has his own version of the famous agreement, which he has been slowly revealing to both the Palestinians and to his own electorate. Neither side are pleased with what they see, but Netanyahu does indeed have his own Oslo blueprint.

The Oslo agreement
When the Declaration of Principles (as the Oslo agreement is officially known[1]) was signed between Yitzhak Rabin and Yasir Arafat on the White House lawn September 13 1993, the intention was to create a framework for negotiations between Israel and the Palestine Liberation Organization (PLO) which would

lead to the end of the conflict. The Oslo accords were revolutionary in providing for the mutual recognition of the State of Israel and the PLO, ending thirty years of mutual denial. The agreement created a three stage process, first a transfer of powers from the Israeli occupation to the Palestinians in undefined territories in Gaza and the Jericho Area, then further Israeli withdrawals and Palestinian elections and finally negotiations which would clarify among other issues 'borders.' While the agreement broadly talked of the legitimate rights of both Palestinians and Israelis, the intention to discuss 'borders' appeared as code for self-determination. At the heart of Oslo was Israeli withdrawal from occupied Palestinian land. As such it struck a blow at the so-called 'national camp' of Israeli politics who viewed the Israeli 1967 occupation of the West Bank as a basis for territorial expansion of the state. Despite the popularity of the agreement amongst most Israelis, in large sections of the right it was seen as betrayal.

Netanyahu, who had become leader of the opposition Likud Party in March 1993, initially opposed Oslo, and over the first years of its implementation was even seen in demonstrations against it. He even went along silently as others denounced Yitzhak Rabin as a traitor. Netanyahu was preparing himself for the first direct elections of an Israeli prime minister which were due in 1996. He realised more than the governing Labour-Meretz coalition that these new elections would be dependent on every single vote and that meant building a political coalition beyond the confines of the Israeli party system. Netanyahu set out to woo the extreme right, the religious constituency, the moderate secular right and the centrist voters who wanted Oslo but who worried about weakening Israel by making too many concessions or moving too quickly. By the time of Rabin's assassination in November 1995 Bibi was ahead in the opinion polls.

By the time of the May 1996 elections, Shimon Peres, Rabin's successor, was busy casting himself in the role of military leader, which was his answer

---

1. There is no one Oslo agreement as such but four key texts: Israel-Palestine Liberation Organisation: Declaration on Interim Self-Government Arrangements, 13 September 1993 ('Oslo"); Agreement on the Gaza Strip and the Jericho Area, 4 May 1993 (the 'Cairo Agreement'); Israeli-Palestinian Interim Agreement on the West Bank and the Gaza Strip, 28 September 1995 ('Oslo 2'); Agreement on Hebron and the Note for the Record, January 1997. For an Israeli-Palestin academic exchange on the Oslo agreements, see Eugene Cotran and Chibli Mallat (eds), *The Arab-Israeli Accords: Legal Perspectives*, Kluwer International Law, 1996.

to the Hamas suicide bombings in the streets of Israel's cities and to the Lebanese Hizbollah's attacks on the northern border. Peres, the man who had coined the phrase 'New Middle East', lost his script during the election and narrowly lost the election to Netanyahu. Bibi had quietly moved to the political centre after Rabin's assassination and refused to denounce Oslo; even more deftly his own manifesto promised to maintain 'all Israel's international agreements'. In interviews he promised that he would meet Arafat 'if it were in the interest of Israel's security'. He even changed track with his electoral slogan 'peace with security' - having assured himself of the religious vote and the right, Netanyahu went towards the centre. Whereas the Likud party declined in its Knesset (Parliament) vote and seats, Netanyahu, the candidate for the prime minister, won by a margin on 27,000 votes, about one half of one per cent.

Bibi's solution

Once in power Netanyahu set about reorganising the approach to the Palestinians. The Israeli left and many outside commentators saw him as the straight anti-Oslo candidate and missed the fact that he had moved towards combining Oslo with his own ideas about the future of Israel, which he advanced in his book, *A Place Amongst the Nations: Israel and the World.*[2] Unlike the most of the right in Israel, Netanyahu understood that Oslo could not be unravelled as it had gone too far in establishing Palestinian facts on the ground. The establishment of the Palestinian Authority and the withdrawal of Israeli jurisdiction from the main population centres meant that the new Israeli prime minister confronted a half-born Palestinian state. Netanyahu thus set out on the road of containing this growing entity and ensuring that if a Palestinian state went to full term it would be the smallest and weakest possible.

In his book, Netanyahu had spelt out his ideas on autonomy for the Palestinians. 'There is no reason,' he writes 'why every lonely cluster of Arab houses should need to claim autonomy over the entire mountain on which it is perched. Thus *autonomy is primarily applicable to urban centres* in which an Arab population can make decisions on day to day life' (p 352).

---

2. Benjamin Netanyahu, *A Place Amongst the Nations: Israel and the World*, Bantam Press, 1993.

Netanyahu sees the Arab population as separate from the land on which they live. This continues the Zionist myth that the Palestinian population is unattached to the land on which they live both emotionally and legally. In this story the Palestinians do not have the identity of a normal people but possess a transitory and itinerant character.

The peculiar identity of the Palestinians becomes a legitimating basis for the appropriation of their land and the establishment of Israeli settlements on it. If the Palestinians can be seen as separate from their land, autonomy becomes a matter of moving a population into the most convenient units for Israeli purposes. For Netanyahu this is underscored by the inherent terrorist threat which is posed by the Palestinians: 'To combat terrorism, Israeli military and security forces must have access to every part of the territory, including the urban centres from which the terrorists may strike and to which they may return for safe haven'. In this account the idea of autonomy is extremely limited and is based on the stereotype of an entire people as terrorists.

Netanyahu's vision of the future of the Palestinians is based on locating the people in tiny territories and subject to Israeli security control. He argues that:

> It would be appropriate, therefore, to develop a system of four self-managing Arab counties: Jenin, Nablus, Ramallah and Hebron. Each of these counties comprise a city and the small towns and villages adjacent to it. Together these counties encompass the great majority of the West Bank's Arab population, and they take up no more than one fifth of the land (p353).

This convenient discovery that most Palestinians live in only about 20 per cent of the West Bank provides the basis for the territorial limitation, in an argument that is similar in tone to the old South African apartheid regime's view that the African population naturally belonged in the 'homeland' which then comprised some 13 per cent of South Africa. However, Netanyahu is willing to go further than Verwoerd as he speculates that 'if the Arabs were to demonstrate clearly that they had adopted a genuine peacetime footing, Israel could consider offering citizenship to the Arab population of Judea and Samaria at the end of a twenty year cooling off period.'

Netanyahu in office

Many journalists and analysts in the international media appeared to have missed reading this book which was published in the same year that Netanyahu became the leader of the Likud. Among many media commentaries it has been conventional wisdom to speculate that the problem with Netanyahu is that he does not know what to do with the peace process.[3] However, a reading of his book is an instructive backdrop to his pronouncements and practices in office. Far from drifting, Netanyahu is engaged in implementing a well thought out plan. He has made this clear in a number of interviews and speeches where he explains that his policy towards the Palestinians is to 'lower expectations'.

In the run up to the May 1996 elections, the result of secret meetings between Labour Cabinet Minister Yossi Beilin and Palestinian negotiator Abu Mazen, including a map detailing the final settlement, were leaked to the press. Both have subsequently denied they had such a map, but few would believe that story. Whether the map was true or not, it seemed a likely outcome of the Oslo process and envisaged that some 90 per cent of the West Bank would be returned to the Palestinians. There would be some territorial adjustments, with about 6 per cent of the West Bank, with the heaviest Israeli settlements (the Etzion bloc South of Jerusalem), being annexed to Israel, and a similar sized tract of desert in the Negev adjacent to Gaza being turned over to the Palestinians. Jerusalem would have remained in Israeli hands, although Palestinians would manage the Islamic holy places, and an area on the edge of the city, Abu Dis, could become the capital of a Palestinian state. The proposal, although falling short of the return of all territory occupied in 1967, was very close, and, most significant of all, it offered the prospect of an independent Palestinian state as the outcome of the peace process. Although this solution had been sought by the international community since the United Nations General Assembly partition resolution 181, in 1947, and reaffirmed in sense in 1967 (in Security Council resolution 242), it was revolutionary for Israeli public opinion. For Netanyahu it represented a major challenge to his colonial-type solution. What concerned him was that Palestinian expectations had been raised to the point that a Palestinian state was on the verge of being achieved.

---

3. See for example Serge Schmemann, 'Outside In', *New York Times Magazine*, 23 November 1997.

In an interview for the popular Israeli TV talk show PopPolitika, Netanyahu argued that he had changed these expectations: 'the most important thing that we did, which gives hope that real peace will be found with the Palestinians, is to lower expectations.'[4] In clarification of this position he explained that he was 'not prepared to accept Palestinian sovereignty... A Palestinian or Arab state here, in the heart of our country, means an Arab army, alliances with Arab countries and dangers.' However he supports the proposition that Palestinians should be able to run their own lives 'without any intervention on our part'. 'I am prepared to give them many powers, but not in areas that can threaten the existence of my country.' In a latter speech in the United States, Netanyahu explained what this meant:

> I have not drawn any precise maps to define what we have in mind for an agreement with the Palestinians. But I do know that I represent a very broad national consensus when I declare that the Jordan Valley must be Israel's strategic border, that Israel will not give up control of airspace and water resources, that it must keep strategic zones that it considers vital; that it will not allow a Palestinian army equipped with heavy weapons or non-conventional arms to form West of the Jordan, and, above all, that Jerusalem will stay the undivided capital of Israel for ever.[5]

Netanyahu's claim that he has no map is inconsistent both with his careful drawing of a geographical picture of the territory of the West Bank that Israel will require, and the much publicised map which has appeared in the press since the summer of 1997. Indeed in his July TV interview he was much less coy about the existence of a map and referred to it as the 'Allon-plus map'. General Allon had produced a plan for Israeli withdrawal from the West Bank in the 1970s, which provided for Israeli control of the Jordan Valley area dividing Israel from Jordan as well as other strategic positions. Netanyahu has worked on this map which was leaked to the press and had

---

4. See Prime Minister Benjamin Netanyahu, Special Interview on Israeli Television, 28 July 1997, *Journal of Palestine Studies*, Vol. XXVII, No 1 (Autumn 1997) p 150.
5. Address by Prime Minister Benjamin Netanyahu to the Council of Jewish Federations General Assembly in Indianapolis, Prime Minister's Reports, Vol. 1 No. 11 (17 November 1997), Prime Minister's Office, Israel.

been widely published. It conforms very largely to Netanyahu's 1993 thoughts on the matter. It divides the West Bank into four areas, three of which are Palestinian, separated from each other - one stretching from Bethlehem to south of Hebron, the Jericho area, and a Northern zone from Ramallah in the south to Jeninin in the North. These three Palestinian zones are intersected by a large Israeli one, which includes occupied East Jerusalem, the Jordan Valley and Judean Desert. The Israeli zone would include nearly all the Israeli settlements, built illegally since 1967, with a combined population, excluding East Jerusalem, of 160,000.

Netanyahu's map contains a narrative which excludes the creation of a contiguous Palestinian territory on which a state could be created. By December 1997 a veritable battle of the maps appeared to have broken out in the Cabinet, with Foreign Minister Levy, Defence Minister Mordechai and Infrastructure Minister Sharon all waving their own versions. However, despite small differences, the maps add up to a small Palestine subject to Israeli security and economic interests.[6]

The current proposals differ in some important respects from those contained in the 1993 book; in particular the proportion of the West Bank ceded to the Palestinians amounts to about 40 per cent and in the place of four counties with self-management there are now three zones, created in the political context of Oslo. Netanyahu's adjustment has been a pragmatic response to the political changes that have been brought about since the signing of the Declaration of Principles in 1993. Despite widespread Palestinian suspicion about the accords, the creation of the Palestinian Authority has drastically changed the situation on the ground. Today the Palestinian Authority is based on the democratic elections held in January 1996 which saw the election of the 88 seat Palestinian Legislative Council and the President of the Authority. This has legitimised the existence of Palestinian political and judicial authorities in the eyes of the Palestinians and the international community. The Authority already runs the main governmental policies for 99 per cent of Palestinians, and it exercises actual jurisdiction over most of the

6. The publication of an apparently common map in the Israeli press makes this very clear, with three areas of the West Bank allocated to the Palestinians, see *Jerusalem Post*, 4 December 1997.

Gaza strip (about 70 per cent) and about 4 per cent of the West Bank. In the latter areas the Authority runs the courts and security apparatus, effectively the Palestinian police and army, a force of some 40,000. In a sense, a form of Palestinian state has already come into existence, a fact symbolised by the powers of the Palestinian Authority to issue internationally recognized passports.[7] The adoption of the Basic Law by the Palestinian Legislative Council is yet another indication of the emergence of the features of a state. These are facts which Netanyahu and the Israeli right wing know they cannot roll back, but think that they can contain.

It has been this that has spurred Netanyahu, ironically, to argue that the Oslo peace process is going too slowly and that he wants to proceed to the permanent status negotiations. In the time~frame established in the Interim Agreement signed in 1995, in the period after the Palestinian elections the Israelis were committed to three further redeployments from the West Bank, leading up to the permanent status negotiations. Under the previous government, it is quite clear that the Palestinian leadership assumed that these further redeployments would leave between 70-80 per cent of the West Bank in the hands of the Palestinians by the time they came to discuss the status of the Palestinian entity, its borders, Jerusalem, settlements and the refugees. This has been one of the expectations that Netanyahu wants to lower drastically. He does not really want to make any serious withdrawal from territory before the final agreement, because his final offer is, as his map indicates, extremely meagre. His first proposal for redeployment amounted to 2.5 per cent of the West Bank. This the Palestinians refused, apparently with the blessing of the Clinton Administration. In November 1997 Netanyahu forced his reluctant cabinet to agree to a further redeployment. This is undoubtedly the result of intense pressure by the Americans who have become irritated by Netanyahu's refusal to push ahead with the agreement. Thus while Arafat seeks meaningful redeployments, Netanyahu wants small ones, so that he can enter the final discussions with the Palestinians in control of perhaps 20 per cent of the West Bank.

Netanyahu and his advisers, in particular the new Israeli UN ambassador

7. See John Whitbeck, ' The Palestinian State Exists', *Palestine-Israel Journal* Vol. III, No. 2, Spring 1996.

Dore Gold and his press chief David Bar Ilan, are attempting to force Yasser Arafat and the Palestinian negotiators into accepting tiny tracts of land with limited powers. Under this plan they play around with the question of whether it would amount to a state or not. In December 1996 David Bar Ilan gave a press briefing in which he referred to a Palestinian entity possessing the powers of Puerto Rico or Andorra. He was apparently horrified to learn that Andorra is now a fully-fledged member of the United Nations. Nevertheless the Israeli right has grasped that Palestinian self-government is unstoppable and they need to get ahead of the momentum in order to shape it. As a result they have begun to speak of the possibility of a state-minus-sovereignty. By this they mean a state without full powers over international relations and in particular barred from making alliances with other Arab states, and naturally a demilitarised entity. It has also become clear, with the demands for the control of vital natural resources, such as water, that they envisage a Palestine economically dependent on Israel. The critical question therefore arises as to whether this policy has any chance.

Obstacles

There are three obstacles to Netanyahu's Oslo - the Palestinians, the American Administration and Israeli politics. The Palestinian leadership has already taken a great risk in negotiating the Accords. The support for the peace process amongst Palestinians has been high at times of momentum, but since the election of Netanyahu has declined. Arafat faces a strong opposition, in particular from the Islamist forces, most obviously from Hamas. In addition, there are the secular and leftist forces which have already rejected Oslo. He cannot afford to be seen to give in to a plan which would reduce Palestine to a permanent local authority with a flag and a passport. This was the outcome predicted by Edward Said, among other opponents of Oslo, at the very beginning.[8] It is for this reason that Arafat and Saeb Erekat his chief negotiator have been very careful to organise political campaigns against all settlements, and in particular on Jerusalem, as a way of demonstrating their radical credentials to the Palestinians in the West Bank and Gaza. A more difficult

---

8. See Edward Said, 'The Morning After', in Edward Said, *Peace and its Discontents*, Vintage 1995.

problem for them is the Palestinian Diaspora, particularly the refugees who have felt excluded by the agreement and who are certainly not part of Netanyahu's solution. Arafat has in fact shown no inclination to deal with Netanyahu and has refused the offer of going straight to the permanent status negotiations. He has, it would appear, read Netanyahu's book.

'Israel is of little importance to the America of the new world order'

The American administration was alarmed by the election of Netanyahu and had publicly backed his opponent, Shimon Peres. In the Autumn of 1997 this alarm turned to hostility, culminating in Bill Clinton's refusal to meet Netanyahu when he visited the United States. Clinton had apparently been outraged by Netanyahu's settlement building activity in Jerusalem, especially the Har Homa project, but had also been startled by the bungled attempt to kill the Amman Hamas spokesperson Masha'al, just days before the sensitive Jordanian elections. In November, Clinton also became acutely aware that perceived closeness to Israel had undermined support in the Arab world for the US policy towards Iraq. This latter event also demonstrates Israel's vulnerability now that the cold war is over and it is no longer a 'front line' state. In reality Israel is of little importance to the America of the new world order. More and more it is becoming an irritant, something which former US Secretary of State James Baker III had famously used expletives about in 1990. The Clinton administration is probably on the verge of changing its policy on the Israeli/Palestinian conflict, and could well opt for the creation of a Palestinian state in the next year, drastically undermining Netanyahu's project.

Israeli politics has been transformed by the innovation of directly electing the prime minister. It has focused power in the hands of the prime minister and at the same time increased the power of smaller political parties. In order to get a majority for his government in the Knesset, Netanyahu was forced to put together a coalition involving his own Likud Party, the three religious parties, one centrist force, and Natan Sharansky's Russian migrants' party. Of this group of 68 members of Knesset, Netanyahu only has the support of 22 Likud MPs (10 others are in alliance with Likud but organise as two public factions). Netanyahu's government is fraught with factional rivalries and conflicting agendas, on which the peace process is only one issue. Nevertheless, it was this government which withdrew from most of Hebron, crossing a red line in the politics of the 'national camp' by withdrawing from the land of Israel. Despite this crossing of the rubicon the government survived. However, opponents of Netanyahu on the right might yet bring him down. He has an ally in Ariel Sharon, the Minister of National Infrastructure (otherwise know as the Butcher of Beirut), who recognised in the early days of Oslo that 'despite the fact that Israel does not want it, a Palestinian state is coming into existence'.[9] Undoubtedly, if Netanyahu survives he and Sharon will work together to contain this coming Palestinian state. However, in Israeli politics the dynamics can change at any movement, and it would be unwise to predict the survival or extinction of any politician.

It is also a challenge to the left, Labour, Meretz and Peace Now! to campaign for their own political vision of peace in the Middle East. With Ehud Barak, Labour's leader, now leading Netanyahu 12 per cent in the opinion polls, it is high time he started to campaign against Netanyahu rather than campaigning like him. Barak's main problem is that he has no real vision of what the peace process might bring the Middle East, unlike his predecessor Shimon Peres. Peres had written about this in his book, *The New Middle East*, published in the same year as Netanyahu's work.[10] In it Peres had speculated about building a close, 'benelux-like' relationship between the Israelis, Palestinians and Jordanians, built on open borders and thus the free movement of capital and people. Barak is much more cautious and is terrified of going ahead of public opinion. Barak, according the journalist Gideon Samat, is rather 'turning himself and his party into something that closely resembles the Likud and its leader'.[11]

Peace Now! has awoken from the shock of Netanyahu's election and has begun to mobilise again. Barak is being drawn into its wake and this could well stiffen his resolve against both Netanyahu and his plans. The massive peace demonstrations in Tel Aviv in September and on the anniversary of Rabin's assassination in November indicate that there is another Israel, which could assert itself against Netanyahu.

---

9. *Jerusalem Post*, 27 November 1997.
10. Shimon Peres, *The New Middle East*, Element 1993.
11. *Ha'aretz*, English edition, 10 December 1997.

The peace threat to Jewish identity

Netanyahu's survival and his plan for the smallest and weakest Palestinian state possible is the result of the maturing of the Jewish political culture of the twentieth century. Netanyahu represents the hesitancy amongst many Jews in Israel and the Diaspora to embrace the peace process with the Palestinians. It is not so much the fear of the threat of the Palestinians or the Arab world as the fear of losing that threat. For much of this miserable century Jews have constituted their identity through the survival of threats to their existence - the Russian pogroms, the shoah, the threats to destroy Israel. The struggle to survive against the enemy has been a fundamental tenet of Jewish consciousness. For the past fifty years, the image of the Jews surrounded by enemies in Israel, and the mobilisation of support for them by the Diaspora, has underlined the Jewish sense of identity. Peace is a threat to Jewish identity as it removes the Other whose threats give it being. Netanyahu's careful honing of the issue of security is not just a political mantra but also fulfills a psychological need. In a strange way it creates a sense of comfort and of home. This is also linked to the attempt to project this tiny Palestinian state. The Palestinians have been constructed as mortal enemies who cannot be treated like other human beings. As Netanyahu reveals in his book, they will use territory not for self-determination but as a basis for terrorist attacks. If they have too much territory they will encourage the refugees to settle them and begin to pressure Israel's existence. The thought of seeing the Palestinians as ordinary neighbours, as Shimon Peres imagined in his book the *New Middle East*, is in this scenario a little threatening.

Benjamin Netanyahu has been forced to begin to speak the language of Oslo. As such he peppers his speeches with talk about each side having to honour its commitments. He will berate the Palestinians with allegations about not cracking down on terrorism, not extraditing terrorists or not altering the Palestinian Covenant. In a strange way this marks a huge leap from the days when all existence of the Palestinians was denied as an article of Zionist faith. The Palestinians have now been constituted in Zionist ideology, even on the right. The Israeli left, Labour, Meretz and Peace Now! have the task of transforming the Palestinians in Israeli discourse into a people possessed of their own inherent rights, like all other peoples. Liberating the Jews from the need to fear the threat to their existence will require a political fight to liberate the Palestinians from Israeli occupation - and colonial imagery.

Five poems

Booking in

Is it the planned feel to it I fear -
the confirmed flight ticket with its carbons' slither?
The letter telling me simply 'You have a bed'?
Is it the vast spaces, the wrap in cloud
and the way gravity rules, and yet is lost?
Either way I know I'll be on my back
pressed into scant upholstery over iron
and someone else will be regulating my breath.
And either way there's only a small resurrection
after it's over, when the retro thrust
reins in the engine and slews the plane to face
the terminal building. Or the reining-in as pain
- the first step to healing, the surgeon says -
tugs me back from cloud to coming round.

Catherine Byron

New Year

Caught in the crossfire of the midnight peal
Dead on the stroke of twelve
Janus looks back, looks forward, does not feel
The rush of angels' wings, the turning wheel
Stone eyes locked on himself.
And so this most momentous moment passes
The clock moves on again: life as it was, is.

Jane Evans

Grandma's winner

In the end the mangle stood
rusting in the back yard,
its tight pressed mouth
I worried I'd trap my fingers in.

They delivered the shiny new spin dryer
one summer in her fifties.
It fitted neatly under the stairs
but more often than not was left
in the dark corner by the kitchenette
and covered with a table-cloth.

She dropped the boiled whites in with wooden tongs.
It made a little popping noise
before she could safely open it,
and out they came, flattened and impressed
with the dryer's patterns.

No more clothes dripping in the shed:
we washed our overalls in the evening
and had them dry by morning.
It liberated her, and us.

But she still stood grappling with the ironing board,
spitting on the iron's tarnished base,
fire-light against her auburn hair.
Between pressing her dresses,
she peered over her glasses, yelling at
Mick MacManus on the Saturday Wrestling
to stop his shenanigans and get up off the mat.

Frances Angela

Mother scrubbing the floor

She had a dancer's feet, elegant, witty.
We had our father's, maverick spreaders of dirt.

Dirt from London, dirt from Kent,
Mud, dust, grass, droppings, wetness, *things*,
Dirt barefaced, dirt stinking, dirt invisible.
Whatever it was, she was ready:
The rubber kneeler, clanking galvanised bucket,
The Lifebuoy, the hard hot water.

Let me! we'd say, meaning *Hate to see you do this.*
Too old. Too resentful. Besides, you'll blame us
That you had to do it.

She never yielded. We couldn't do it right,
Lacking her hatred of filth, her fine strong hands.

Don't want you to do this, she said. *Don't want you to have to.*
Just remember this: love isn't sex
But the dreary things you do for the people you love.
And 'Home is the girl's prison,
The woman's workhouse,' Not me; Shaw.

I do remember. I stand where she knelt.

U.A. *Fanthorpe*

High rise flat

Up here with binoculars I used to watch
small white packets change hands -
conjurers, palming. Then
they'd piss in coke tins on the footbridge
and cool down cyclists.
But knives ... that's different.

So I went to the RSPCA, chose a manky scrap,
paws big as lily pads, and fed him up -
tinned soup, bacon rind, leftovers from the fridge.
To start with he'd wolf the lot, then be sick.

I taught him everything. Manners
and that; not to lick his balls
when I brought birds back.
He'd have jumped off the balcony
to retrieve the moon if I'd trained him to.

Only thing he never got the hang of
was the lifts. He liked them Out of Order.
Both of them.
He sussed that one was for the odd floors
(no good to us) but whenever I dived in the other
he'd follow all right.

If I slithered out just as the doors shut
he'd be trapped like a cockroach in a matchbox;
by the time they opened automatically I'd have legged it
halfway up to the 12th floor. He'd chase,
slathering, straight from hell. Drove him mad.

Sometimes I'd press the wrong button,
all innocent, and wait.
Soon as we arrived he knew something was up,
but couldn't tell which way to jump.
I'd make a dash, then halt
and watch him lollop up or down a flight, stop,
wheel round ...
There were times on the landing
when he'd look me in the eye and growl
before I'd even made a move.

He had other ways of getting me back;
streetwise, he'd pull one leg after the other.

Gregory Warren Wilson

Karomat Isaeva's tale

as told to Colette Harris

My name is Karomat Isaeva.[1] I was born in November 1925 in my mother's native village of Zarkhok (which means golden earth), in Leninabad province.[2] My mother was born in 1905. My father was born in 1903 in another part of Leninabad. He came from an old clerical family and went to study in the town. Afterwards he was sent to work in my mother's village. He saw my mother about in the village and fell in love with her. He asked her parents to give her to him in marriage and they agreed. They were married in 1924. Before they married she did not love him but afterwards she came to do so. In all, my mother gave birth to ten children - four boys and six girls. I was the oldest. Of the earliest children only myself and my second sister, born in 1927, survived. A third sister, born in 1937, and my two youngest sisters, born after World War II, also survived. All the boys died. My parents lived together for over 70 years, during which time they were never apart.[3] My mother died in October 1992,

---

1. This work is based on three field trips to Tajikistan, made between December 1994 and June 1995, December 1995 and February 1996, and from January to July 1997. I want to thank the many women who shared their lives with me and especially Karomat, who adopted me into her own family and whose friendship and love greatly enriched my time in her country. I interviewed her many times during my two and a half years in the country and she told me many details of her life and that of her family and friends. Although in her seventies Karomat's memory remained excellent and she had forgotten little that had happened to her since early childhood. What follows are, as nearly as possible in her own words, some extracts from her life story.
2. This is the Northern part of Tajikistan, which has now reverted to its historical name of Hujant.
3. Except for when her father served in the army.

Above: Karomat Isaeva (left) with her Russian friend Bella, in 1997.

Right: The faranja.

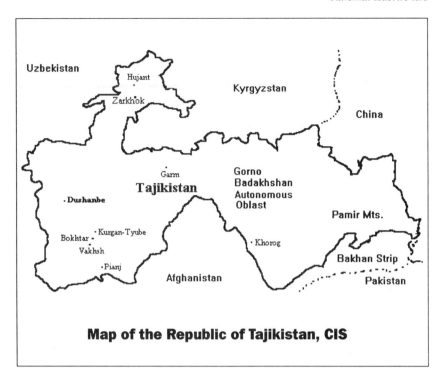

Map of the Republic of Tajikistan, CIS

just as the war began in Dushanbe;[4] my father was most unhappy without her. He died in December 1995.

My mother's childhood (1905-1924)

My mother used to love to tell us tales of her life before she was married, before she left home and went to work with the communists. In those days they had all the food they wanted; most of it they provided themselves. They had sheep, so they always had meat. There were fruit trees, a vegetable garden, rice fields, and so on. The village has mountains on one side and a river on the other.

When my mother was young she and her friends would go down to the river. They could not swim but made a shallow bathing place for themselves where they could go and take off their clothes. They used to be sent to the river

___

4. The capital of Tajikistan.

to collect water which they would carry on their hips in earthenware jars.

In those days girls did not get to choose whom they married. Their parents made all decisions for them. But some girls managed to fall in love somehow and even at times to get pregnant. Nowadays when they have problems girls hang themselves or pour petrol over themselves and set it alight.[5] In my mother's youth unhappy girls would throw themselves into the river.

Once my mother even saw this happen. The girl's parents had chosen a rich suitor rather than the poor man with whom she had fallen in love. When her parents had ordered her to marry the rich man, the girl walked into the river; further and further she walked until the water was above her head and she vanished. All the village girls were there bathing at the time. When this girl came into the water and went on and on wading out, all the girls begged and begged her not to go any further; but she didn't listen. After that their parents wouldn't let the girls go near the river for at least a year.

If a girl got pregnant the village elders would assemble, together with the local judge and religious leaders. They would stone the girl to death and then bury her. The boy was never even punished. He may have loved her and wanted to marry her but he would not be allowed to.

Unmarried girls would wear a white cloak over their heads. If a man came near, they would cover their face on the side the man was. If there were men on both sides they would pull the cloak over both sides of their face with both hands. Only after they married did women wear the full face veil under the cloak (see illustration).

Generally, life was good in those days, much better than later. Women were women and men men, and each knew their place and didn't try to usurp each other's functions. Each person - father-in-law, mother-in-law, husband, wife, had their own place and filled their proper function. Women stayed at home, gave birth to their children, cooked, did the housework, gossiped together, went to weddings, and generally had a good time. Men rarely beat their wives; they feared God and the neighbours and behaved themselves.

---

5. During the last years of the Soviet Union there were many stories in the press about girls and women in Central Asia immolating themselves.

The Bolsheviks and Tajik women

The Soviet state found it vital for its survival to incorporate the women as well as the men into their revolution. It was not so hard to do this for the Russian women, but the Muslim women of Central Asia were much harder to reach, especially those who lived secluded from society, covering themselves when in the presence of strange men.

In the mid 1920s the Bolsheviks started a campaign to liberate these women from seclusion, polygyny, child marriage, and other local customs. However, despite the propaganda, they did this not so much for the sake of the women themselves but in order to achieve specific political ends - namely to bring both the women and the men of Central Asia into compliance with the Soviet state.

At the same time the stories of women's lives all over the USSR show their resistance to the state and the way they were able to subvert the processes that the government was aiming for. This is nowhere more evident than in Central Asia and especially Tajikistan. Here the women took great care to preserve their own culture although at the same time they did take on some of the greater personal freedoms provided them by the state.

The early years of Bolshevism (1924-1941)

My mother and her friends unveil

Then the communists came and forced us to change our way of life. On 8 March, International Women's Day - it must have been the year 1930 or 1931 - just around the time the collective farm was being set up, the farm's director warned the women that the next day there would be a big meeting and they should be ready to burn their *faranjas*.[6] I was five years old at the time and I remember it vividly. My father and I often discuss those days now and he can't believe I really remember everything. But I do. I remember practically everything that has happened to me since I was four years old. I can certainly never forget the

---

6. Literally cloaks. The word *faranja* is often used to denote not just the cloak but also the *chachvan* or horsehair veil that covered the entire head and face, without even eye holes (see illustration).

day when my mother removed her *faranja*.

They brought women from several villages together and one-by-one they had to throw their *faranjas* on a big fire that had been built there.[7] As each woman threw her *faranja* on the fire she was greeted with the words 'Happy Women's Day'. Those women who didn't want to burn their *faranjas* were made to, all the same. They would take them off still desperately holding on to them. Then the Soviet men would forcibly pull the *faranja* from them. This made some women even fall on the floor, as they were holding on to the *faranja* so tightly. These women were not greeted because they had not done what they were told. Once their *faranjas* had been burned, they slunk away, trying to cover themselves as best they could.

The reason for their terror was that they knew that their menfolk would punish them, might even kill them. Many girls and women who took off their *faranjas* were stoned to death because it was considered anti-Islamic and therefore wrong.[8]

After all the *faranjas* had been burned they had a feast at which all the women who had removed their *faranjas* voluntarily, including my mother of course, sang and danced.

While the women were sitting there by the bonfire a tractor came into the village. It had been sent as a present from the Bolsheviks. Never before had they seen such a monster. In it came, belching smoke and roaring away like a wild beast, and all the women were terrified. They thought it would attack them and tear them to shreds. My sister and I were sitting there with our mother, scared to death also.

The following day all the women looked like plucked chickens. They could not get used to being exposed to the sight of men and would cover themselves with their headscarves. For some time, those older women who just couldn't get used to going without their *faranja* would wear a man's shirt thrown over their heads. They would draw it round their faces if a man

---

7. Similar scenes took place all over those parts of Central Asia where women were veiled, mostly Northern Tajikistan and Southern Uzbekistan. There are published accounts of the ceremonies in the major cities, such as Tashkent, when thousands of women burned their *faranjas* on one day, often to put on another one the next! This unveiling was a major part of Soviet strategy in the area.
8. Perhaps as many as 1000 women and men were killed during the course of the whole unveiling movement, and many more punished in other ways.

Left:
A younger
Karomat
Isaeva

appeared. But gradually everyone got used to going unveiled. My own mother wore a large white headscarf and tied it behind her head.

Once they had removed their cloaks and veils there was nothing preventing the women from going to work just like the men. In fact, this was the time that they were setting up the collective farm, much against everyone's will, and they needed women to work in the fields. They would have to work all day on the farm, and then go home in the evening when they were already tired, and do all the housework they had previously spent the whole day on. Then they would have to get up the following day and go to work again without any free time. The men got off lightly; they never did any work in the house. On the contrary, they would expect to be waited on hand and foot when they came home. My father expected our mother to take his boots off and immediately give him food no matter what time he arrived. He lived in our house like a guest.

My parents study to be Communists

In 1929 my father had been taken into the army. He was released the following year, which was when the collective farm was formed in the village. My parents were the most active couple on the new farm. Although my father came from a learned Muslim family he realised that it was no use resisting and trying to stick with the old ways. If he wanted to get on, he would have to join the communists. This was when the collective-farm leadership were looking round for the right people to send to Dushanbe to study; my parents were picked. They didn't do anything active to be chosen. They were just given the option of going or not. So they went and they took us children with them. My mother was to be trained as a teacher and my father as a party official.

Their school had a dormitory building for those families who were there for just a short while. They also had a kindergarten and crèche. I and my sister went to the kindergarten and our baby brother to the crèche. Both were right there on the grounds of our parents' school. We lived there all week, staying with our parents only at weekends. All we girls were dressed alike, in Russian-style trousers in winter, and shorts in summer both over short skirts, and we wore headscarves. Most of the teachers were Russian women so this is where I first started learning the language. We were taught how to sit on chairs - something we never did at home, where we sat on the floor. And we did drawing and other things. We were taught how to behave in the correct (Russian) way. Our mother used to come in and see us whenever she could, usually two or three times a day.

My parents start their work for communism

We remained in Dushanbe for three years. Then my parents were sent to start working in rural areas in the South. My father would start a new Party organisation in a village while my mother would set up a school there. Every two to three years we would all move to a different place because of my father's Party work. As soon as he had introduced the concepts of the Party and socialism in one place he would be sent to the next.

E very time we arrived in a new village all the women would come out and stare at us. My mother didn't cover her face. She worked as a teacher. The local women didn't wear *faranjas* like Northern women. Northern women would get home and take off their *faranja* and be in indoor dress. Southern women wore clothes that almost completely covered them all the time, indoors and out. They covered their heads and faces with large headscarves, until only their eyes were visible. Their dialects were so different from what we were used to in the North that at first we couldn't understand each other.

For the first while all the women would do nothing but stare at us and listen to us. We were not really like a Tajik family any more. My sister and I wore our hair very short and in the beginning the village women would never be able to decide whether we were girls or boys. Our family had a gramophone - something totally unheard of in Tajikistan at the time. We would put on records and dance to them. The whole village would be spellbound by this and the other interesting things about our family. We would often speak Russian at home, which none of them could understand. Also, we had lived in many different places while most villagers had never been more than a few kilometres from home.

B ut it was also very difficult to be constantly in new places and among new people whose customs and even dialects we didn't know. It was especially hard for me. At first in each new place I really hated it. I didn't like it when everyone stared. It would take two or three months before I would get to know the other girls and begin to have a couple of friends. Another problem was schooling. I had already finished my first year of school in Dushanbe, but whenever we came to a new place where there had been no school before, my mother would have to start another first year. This meant that there was no class for me to go to. So I ended up staying home and doing most of the housework. I was rarely allowed to spend time with my friends outside the house. My mother was teaching school for the village children in the daytime and running literacy courses for adults at night, so she had no time for domestic work. By the time I was 12 years old I was as good at it as my mother because I had been helping out since I was six. It was my responsibility also to look after the children. If any of them cried, my mother would always blame me. But I didn't really mind that. I adored my mother and anything she said was fine by me. Her word was always law for me.

Then, just as I would get a couple of good girlfriends and begin to feel at home somewhere, we would move again. This continued until I was 15 years old and we moved back to Dushanbe, where I have lived almost ever since. But I have never felt that I was able to make the same sort of really, really close friend of my own age that I might have had if I had grown up in one place. Now I am old and really feel the lack of a few close women friends. It still makes me so upset to think of my childhood and all that moving around. I cannot bear to think too much about it.

World War II and immediately after (1941-1950)
Life without father

In 1941 my father was conscripted into the army again; this time he was sent to the European war front. When he went to train in Dushanbe he took us with him. All schools were closed down for the duration except for specialist trade schools. The men were needed at the front or in other wartime employment and there were hardly any women teachers in Tajikistan at that time.

At first we lived in a dormitory building. When my father left for the front we bought a house with a courtyard, where we lived for the rest of the war. We had our own vegetable garden so we didn't do too badly for food. My father sent us all his pay by post. However, we still needed more money because my mother was not working and there were altogether five of us children. My father's pay would cover our bread ration and pay for flour, oil, and other foods - in any case there was little in the shops to buy at that time - but it was not sufficient for us to buy clothes and other necessities as well, so I had to go out to work.

Everyone over the age of 13 was supposed to work, anyway. A family registered as residents in a specific place got a bread ration, the size of which depended on the number of children they had.[9] But those who moved to town from the provinces didn't have a bread ration; the only way to get ration

---

9.   Bread is the staple food in Tajikistan.

coupons was to go to work, so most people did. The only exception was the women from Dushanbe itself, very few of whom worked.

My war work at home in Tajikistan

Everyone possible was sent to the front and all work was directed only towards the war effort. In the factories and other workplaces we worked specially long shifts. We went in early in the morning and never looked at the clock, working until the lunch gong sounded. Then in the evening we went on until we were told - you can go home now. During this whole time we had no free days, no weekends off, at all. I worked at first in the silk factory and later as a lab assistant in a scientific laboratory. I really liked the last place a lot although I was the only Tajik woman working there. All the others were Russians. But they were very nice to me.

At the weekend either we went into work as usual or else we were asked to do other work to help the war effort. For instance, I helped dig the Varsovsky canal. We did this all without machinery. I was young and strong and didn't mind it. We would dig and dig and while we dug we would sing. At lunch time people would play musical instruments too and we would really enjoy ourselves. We would get there and back in trucks. There were mostly Tajiks digging. The Russians did other things.

We would also pick fruit and vegetables in season. There were not enough people on the land to do this, especially with all the young men at the front. We would pick as fast and as much as we could. Then a plane would come and we would load everything on to it and it would all be taken to Moscow. We didn't get any of the produce for Tajikistan. It all went to Russia.

Picking cotton

But the most important work we were asked to do was to pick cotton.[10] We would start work in the very early morning when it was just getting light and continue until lunch-time. Then we would start again in the late afternoon until around 9 p.m. Cotton is white and can be easily seen in the half light. If

---

10. In fact, cotton remained vital for the Soviet economy, and even after World War II there were never enough agricultural workers to pick the cotton, so they would rope in school children and students. This continued almost up to the end of the Soviet period.

there were a moon we could pick even longer.

Lunch-time lasted three hours since it was impossible to pick in the heat of the day. During it we would sing songs. Sometimes we would go off and try to find fruit somewhere and pick enough to eat and even some to take home with us. We especially liked water melons. Sometimes we would load the trucks up with so much fruit we had nowhere to sit.

Children as young as eight years old would be sent to pick the cotton. The smaller ones were so short they could not be seen above the tops of the cotton plants. You would just see the plants swaying and know there was a young child picking there.

'I helped dig the Varsovsky canal - we did it all without machinery'

I would try to be one of the very best pickers and get the most praise and a medal. Each picker had to have her cotton weighed and the amounts were noted and then added up at the end of the day. We used a number of tricks to get the cotton to seem to weigh more. Some of the women put stones in with it - sometimes as much as 5-6 kg. But when the cotton was poured out of the baskets the stones would be visible. I had a better way. I would fill a basket, then put it down on the wettest ground I could find, while I was filling the next one. Then I would pick up the first one which was now quite wet and take it to be weighed. It would weigh much heavier than it really was. In this way I was able to make a record of 120 kg in a day. In fact, I once picked that much even without wetting it.

But we were not the only ones to cheat. The man weighing the cotton would also do so.[11] He would try to write down fewer kilograms than the real weight. This would make me very angry. If any of them tried it on me I would immediately tell him I was going to report him. This would really frighten him and he would beg me not to and tell me it was just a mistake. But after one time he would not try it on again with me.

I get married
When I was 17, the government began to send unmarried girls to the front as nurses. I absolutely did not want to go. We had a family conference and it was

---

11. Then as now, it was the women who did the hard physical labour of picking and the men who took the easier work of weighing the cotton, and other supervisory tasks.

decided I should get married. As it happened, I did have a boyfriend at that time. We had known each other since I was 15; he was a couple of years older. He had failed his medical and so had not been sent to the front to fight. We had courted for those two years, gone to the cinema together and so on. That is, I would go with a group of girlfriends and he with a group of boyfriends and perhaps we could get a quick word together on the way home. We did not behave like Russians, meeting freely and without shame.

He wanted to marry me and I was in favour of this. My mother agreed. My father would most likely not have agreed had he been at home. In that case I would probably have been married off to someone he chose for me. That might have been better. I don't know. It is good to obey your parents. But my father wasn't there and I did marry my friend. I don't regret it but the one bad thing was that this meant I was never able to finish school. I was already married when the war finished and the schools reopened. All my sisters were able to study but my husband would not let me do the same, however much I begged him. He told me he had no use for an educated wife. I would only go to the bad. He was a skilled man himself, a lorry driver.

We only did *nikoh*; we did not register our marriage with ZAGS.[12] We managed to get away with this because of the war. Before and after it the authorities penalised any *mullahs* (clerics) who celebrated *nikoh* and would throw them in prison if they were caught, but during the war they did not do this.

Even after my marriage I had, of course, to keep on working even though I was pregnant a lot of the time. It was only in the late 1940s that we were allowed to stop the war effort. After that my husband didn't want me to work any more. He wanted me to stay home and be there when he came back from work, although, in fact, he was not around very much. His job was to drive a lorry from Dushanbe to Khorog, which could take as much as ten days there and back. [13]

After the war few soldiers came home. So many had died. We were lucky that my father did come back. He was sent to another part of the provinces and my family moved away from Dushanbe with him, leaving me behind with my husband and in-laws.

---

12. *Nikoh* is the Muslim marriage ceremony. ZAGS is the official civil registry office.
13. Khorog is in the Pamir mountains. It is the capital of the Autonomous Province of Mountainous Badakhshan.

My parents-in-law the *Beys*[14] (1900-1950)

My husband's family came from a very different background from mine. My mother-in-law was born around 1898-1900 in a village not far from Dushanbe. At the age of 15 she was married forcibly to a cousin whom she didn't like. She had practically to be forced by the *mullah* to sleep with her husband. After the first time she categorically refused to sleep with him or even go near him again. She hid away and that was that.

After several months they realised it was hopeless and she went back to her family. Shortly after that, a rich man, who had a sort of country place in the village, saw my mother-in-law-to-be and thought that she was extremely beautiful. He gave a lot of money for *kalym* (bride price) for her to marry him. She agreed because he was very good looking and she fell for him.

He took her to live with him in Dushanbe. Their women's quarters had three rooms. In each of the first two rooms was a woman she was told to call *apa* (elder sister). The third room was hers. One woman had a rather sickly son. No-one explained anything to her. She did what the *apas* told her and did the house work. The other two women were considerably older than she was.

The first few nights her husband spent with her. But eventually one night he didn't come to her room. In the morning he came to breakfast and she asked him where he had spent the night. He got furious at her and said - who is the husband, you or I? Don't you dare ask me such a question ever again. So she shut her mouth and kept quiet. She told me it would have been better if he had hit her than said such words and looked at her with such cold eyes.

Then gradually she worked it out. She had vaguely heard that some men had several wives and went to them in turn. She realised that this was the case here. The other two women turned out to be his first two wives. He would sleep with all three in strict rotation and treat them alike. Whenever her husband gave something to one wife, he would give the others exactly the same. The boy called him father. So they all lived together amicably. She was never formally told that these other women were his wives. In her village no-one knew about it and she didn't dare ask anyone in Dushanbe because she had no family of her own there. The only people she knew were her husband's relatives who would be bound to lie to her.

---

14. *Beys* were the Tajik equivalent of rich landowners.

Every year she bore a child. In all she had twelve. Ten of them died. Two boys lived. My husband was called *sang* (stone) because they cut the umbilical cord with a stone not a knife and so he lived.

And so their life went on. Then the Soviets came to Dushanbe and everything changed.[15] Her husband was a rich man and therefore his lands, houses, and all other property were confiscated. He was sent off to exile along with his whole family. In the middle of one winter they were simply dumped in the Caucasus. The place they were sent to was very cold. They were given tents to live in. They tried to cultivate the land to produce food but they could not really produce enough. Every month an aeroplane flew over and dropped them foodstuffs and other necessities. That was all the contact they had with the outside world. There were no roads, and no trains.

Many, many people died, including the two first wives and the sickly son. My father-in-law became brigadier - after all, he was used to being boss. They remained there for two years. Then the Bolsheviks told them they were free to return home. Most people didn't want to go. They were frightened that they would get there only to have to return.

But my parents-in-law came back to Dushanbe. On their arrival they had nowhere to live. All their property had been confiscated. My father-in-law's relatives were too frightened to take them in. They didn't know for sure that they might not have run away and what the Bolsheviks might do to anyone who took them in. So they would only allow them to sleep in a cattle-shed at first, until it was confirmed that they had permission to return. Eventually they got work on a collective farm and managed to get a little land and a two-roomed house. This is where my mother-in-law and husband were living when I met him and where we spent my married life.

My husband and his second wife still live in this house, while, since the death of my parents, I have lived alone in a small two-room flat in the centre of town, that was allocated to me when I worked at the textile factory.

Karomat Isaeva died on 5 November 1997, only a few days before her 72nd birthday.

---

15. Owing to the strong resistance put up by the locals they did not arrive until the mid 1920s.

Biographical Note

Karomat was the only member of her family not to have completed school nor to have had a professional career. She always regretted her lack of formal education. Although she managed to pick up a great deal of knowledge, she felt that she does not have the intellectual tools that would enable her to make the best use of it. At the same time she was an immensely strong and forceful woman, unafraid of carrying out tasks usually left to men, such as making bricks to build her house, painting her own flat when well into her sixties, and so on. She was also capable of taking on Soviet officials and often beating them at their own game.

Unfortunately, her lack of education and a real profession left her in her old age without any meaningful goals. While still part of the conscripted labour force shortly after World War II, she had an ineptly treated miscarriage and, as a result, was unable to conceive any more. Her earlier children had previously died, of measles and other infant diseases. This left her childless in a society where children are by far the most important assets anyone can have. Refusing to adopt, unable eventually to face up to the pressures of her in-laws, although much against her husband's will, Karomat eventually left him to return home to her own parents at the age of nearly 38.

She subsequently went to work in the huge Dushanbe textile factory, where she remained for over 20 years. Meanwhile she looked after her parents single-handedly until their recent deaths at the age of over 90. Since that time she lost much of her previous vigour, feeling she was useless and needed by no-one, especially her younger and far more successful sisters.

Upset at the idea that she would leave nothing behind her when she died, no children and no renown, Karomat had long been thinking that she might get someone to help her ghost her autobiography. She saw my appearance in her life as the fulfilment of her need for some sort of recognition. For this reason, unlike the other women I have interviewed, she insisted I use her real name when I write about her.

The perverse modernisation of British universities

Michael Rustin

The conception of 'modernisation' being imposed on British universities seems to mean only so-called efficiency gains, competitive stratification through league tables, and students having to fund their own education as an investment in their future. This article argues that the virtues of the British system lie in its high quality, its intensity of teaching, and the broad scope of its educational mission. A truly 'modern' approach would seek to make the most of these qualities, not to undermine them.

We need to see the extreme pressures now being faced by the British university system in the light of the general restructuring of the public sector which was undertaken by the Conservative governments from 1979. Universities are being subjected to a regime of defunding, competition, intensified stratification, and ultimate privatisation, just as one can see similar processes in operation in other public services, such as broadcasting, health, and the school system. The underlying trends and choices have to be recognised, if the erosion or reversal of democratic provision is to be avoided.

The restructuring of the British public sector

The 'revolutionary' character of Thatcherism was of course most obvious in its decisive confrontations with the forces and institutions of the working class. Its legislative attack on trade unions, their defeats in decisive battles such as that of the 1984-85 miners' strike, the abandonment of full employment, and the weakening of the 'social guarantees' provided by the welfare state in its various aspects, were all clear enough in both their intention and effect.

However, the Thatcherite regime was equally radical in its strategy for restructuring almost the entire public sector of British institutional life. This was most obvious in its programmes of privatisation of hitherto public industries and utilities. Here it has set a path-breaking example for countries in different phases of economic development, privatisation proving to be a highly exportable invention.

But no less significant has been the transformation of those large parts of the public sector which have remained publicly owned or funded. Among the key reform programmes here are the instituting of 'internal markets' in the National Health Service, the development of a 'contract culture' within local government, the hiving-off of many former civil service functions to independent agencies, and the imposition of contracting-out and of a managerialist culture and method in the BBC under the regime of John Birt.

The aim of this reform programme has been both to create private market involvement in the provision of public services, wherever this is feasible (e.g. in the contracting out of local government services or the production of television programmes to private providers) and to create 'quasi-markets' even where 'full marketisation' was politically or for other reasons impossible. The 'purchaser-provider' split inside the NHS is one large example of this methodology, and it has many other analogues and equivalents. Another dimension has been the attempt to introduce an equivalent of 'consumer sovereignty' into public service provision. This has nearly always taken the individualist form of enlarged 'consumer choice' rather than the more collectivist form of greater consumer representation - in Hirschman's terms, enhancing 'exit' rather than 'voice'.[1]

The explicit or implicit enemies, in this revolution in public provision, have been two overlapping systems and cultures. One of these is the forms of bureaucratically-organised provision mandated by the political process, funded by taxation, and implemented through state bureaucracies. These have been deemed to be inefficient, monopolistic, and inherently biased in their values against the free market. The second of these is the system and culture of professionalism, the provision of public services, on behalf of the state or the community, by largely self-regulating professional providers, such as the professions working within the NHS, or the schoolteachers. 'Professionalism', in this neo-conservative way of thinking, has been deemed to be inherently self-serving, little more than a trade unionism of the middle class.

So a national curriculum and external assessments have been imposed on the schools, devolved budgets (and the competitive mentality they unavoidably generate) on every public service provider from schools to GPs, and a managerialist form of both centralisation and hiving-off on to the BBC, supplanting a culture hitherto notable for its ethos of management by those with proven professional expertise in the various disciplines of programme-making.

It seems likely that this quasi-marketised public sector, in which auditors, accountants, and managers assume newly dominant roles over the specialist professionals of each sector, was intended to be merely an unstable transitional stage in the construction of a divided system, one part of which would operate in as near as possible to a full market environment (where it was not privatised entirely), and the other part of which would constitute a residual sector of public provision for those who could afford nothing better. This would be subject to authoritarian forms of control, legitimised in the name of 'standards' but also bearing a good deal of unconscious hostility to public provision and its indigent publics. We can see the spirit of this residual public sector to come in the 'tough' approach taken to failing schools and their teachers, even where the failure of some such schools is an unavoidable product of large-scale social neglect.

One reason, apart from the ideological agendas which underly these

---

1. Albert Hirschman, *Exit, Voice and Loyalty*, Harvard Unversity Press, 1970.

developments, for inferring a full-market destination for public sector institutions, is the climate of continuous defunding in which they have almost all been obliged to operate. If what is available on a universalistic, tax-funded basis fails to keep up with user expectations, or indeed with the improvements in standards continually experienced within the market sector, consumers will be progressively forced out of the public system, or at the least to supplement it with top-up private provision.

David Elstein remarked some months ago (he then worked for Sky TV) that the satellite companies had noticed that the terrestrial licence fee had been set 'too low', too low that is to fund the quality and range of services that audiences wanted. (This in spite of the dramatic economies of scale which are realised through a system of universal free access to broadcasting.) This gap, between the optimal licence fee from the point of view of service provision, and the actual licence fee charged, is what has created the space for 'top-up' private provision by satellite and cable broadcasters. But of course, the BBC's licence-fee is neither an accident, nor set by the BBC itself, but is decided by government. It is obvious that the inadequacy of the licence fee to meet the BBC audience's demand for services has been determined on purpose, both to necessitate Birt's internal market reforms, and to create space in which the subscription-based competition can flourish.

Very similar mechanisms have been set up in most other fields of provision. Under-funding of health, or dentistry practice, forces consumers into private provision. Under-funding of pensions requires investment in occupational or private schemes. Poor public transport increases the relative attractiveness of the car, etc.

With remarkable boldness, and probably cynicism, the government that had created the conditions in which at least relative if not absolute standards were bound to fall, at the same time began to insist that standards were important, and that consumers must be given more power to insist on them. The era of the Citizens' Charters was born, for NHS patients, university students, schoolchildren's parents, and even rail travellers. We were all given the right to say what was the matter with the services provided for us, and a new form of persecution of the professional providers of those services was invented. Whilst in principle there is much to be said for enhanced 'customer voice', its main function in this period was to give more power to higher level managers over the lower-level providers of services, and to give a new weapon to the ubiquitous inspectors and auditors. It also served to create impatience with the services themselves, in circumstances in which their general improvement was all but impossible. The effect was to visibly stratify them, the 'league tables' for schools and universities appearing as the visible register of these new competitive hierarchies.

The General Election of 1 May 1997 was in large part a plebiscite about whether this revolutionary dismantlement (or at least stratification prior to dismantlement) of the public sector should continue on its course or not. This was one reason why the health service and education were such central election issues, since these remain the largest nearly-universal public services. (They also remain, in autumn 1997, the main objects of public anxiety.) The Conservatives' falling-out with the professions had

'A broad and inclusive educational mission is now under severe threat'

reached the point by the election when they were openly quarrelling not only with the BMA and the teachers' unions, which was only to be expected, or even with the clergy (now the main voices of the very poor in British society), but with the prison governors and with the judges, neither hitherto noted for their liberal sympathies.

The Conservatives, of course, lost, and lost badly. It should follow therefore that the crusade against the public sector, and against the professionalised forms of service-provision which flourish within it, should have been halted. However, it has become clear that the changes set in motion by Thatcherism retain a momentum of their own, and it is by no means clear that a new direction has yet been, or will now be, set. The taxation and expenditure targets set by the previous government, and accepted by new Labour, impose impossible limits to doing anything really different, that is to the reconstruction of universally-acceptable public services. These limits enforce a regime of 'posthumous Thatcherism', and the resort to disciplinary measures (in 'welfare to work', toughness on crime, and no more than a month's tolerance of poor teachers) only display a need for government to be doing *something* when it finds it impossible to do what is really necessary. 'Toughness' in other words, has the same diversionary function for new Labour as it had for its predecessor in office. It seems to hold the immediate providers of public services responsible for their failings, even when the causes lie in larger scarcities which are enforced by government.

The universities

The university sector exemplifies many of the pressures and contradictions which can be seen elsewhere in the public sector. An educational mission which has grown increasingly broad and inclusive since the post-Robbins expansion is now under severe threat, and the re-stratification and perhaps privatisation of part of this system is now being placed on the agenda by forces beyond the universities' control. The universities had over many years already acquired many of the attributes of a well-functioning 'internal market'. Funding came largely through taxation, via grants administered by the University Grants Committee and its equivalents for the public sector, and via student grants and notional full-time fees paid in fact by the state. In this respect, it was and remains a public system. But students competed for places, on the basis of their various merits and qualifications, and universities competed for students, offering their resources of quality, environment and prestige to attract the most valued student body. Universities competed also for research funding, in various public and private research markets. The severity of this competitive regime, in the period before 1979, was mitigated by the system of quinquennial grants, and by the fact that for many years priority was given to expansion rather than efficiency.

This 'quasi-market' system is the modernised legacy of the universities' original independence from central government. The universities have formed part of a substantial 'civil society', supported by endowments by aristocracy and later by the industrial bourgeoisie, and in the case of the great civic universities by municipal governments. The 'public sector' created by Crosland in 1976 remained formally under the control of local authorities, even though virtually all of its funding came from central government. The academic autonomy conferred on universities by these devolved forms of control has given some protection to academic autonomy, and has probably also been more supportive of innovation and differentiation than university systems such as those of France or Italy which are tightly regulated by central government.

From the late 1970s, the claims of the higher education system for ever more resources to fund the growth of student numbers became a problem for governments. The 'binary system' was established by the Labour government ostensibly as a stimulus to 'useful knowledge', but in reality more to facilitate the expansion of the higher education system at much lower unit costs than were then acceptable to the older universities. The polytechnics and colleges - after 1992 the 'new universities' - proved highly responsive to financial inducements to expand student numbers, enabling governments to meet the demands for places from students and parents which have remained the most potent driving force of the system throughout this period. The government devised other market disciplines for the university system. For example the quinquennial funding round turned into an annual funding allocation, until it became decided to institute 'efficiency gains' on a three-year rolling basis. (This was a return to a form of medium-term planning but only in its most negative form.) The raising of overseas student fees to full-cost levels (at first controversial) forced universities into a new competitive market. The validation and quality-audit system of the Council for National Academic Awards (CNAA) was brought under pressure to impose more competitive and stratifying standards. When its academic membership proved reluctant to go along with this, it went the way of the HMI and was abolished for reason of its loyalty to its professional constituency. The regime of self-regulation which remained acceptable for the City was rejected by government for the professional sphere of higher education.

These pressures on the system, in the direction of internal marketisation and external control, were consolidated in the Education Reform Act of 1992. This Act offered the former polytechnics membership of a unified university sector, (undoubtedly an advance for them from the previous two-tier system). But it also strengthened the regime of audit and competition, with a universal system of 'teaching quality assessment' and 'research assessment' applying to the 'old' as well as the 'new' universities and colleges. These systems rapidly became digitalised, with a points and grades system making it easy to construct hierarchies of quality on each dimension. These were readily translated into more or less vulgarised 'league tables' of quality, exactly paralleling the outcomes of standard assessments for the school system.

At the same time as they were being made more publicly accountable through various regimes of audit and inspection, universities were also asked to become more accountable to their 'customers', the students, via Student Charters, formalised complaints procedures and the like. All these systems had costs attached to them, not least in diverting effort from the primary tasks of teaching, research, and the support of a learning environment, to the secondary tasks of meeting the requirements of the audit systems. I think it is likely that innovation and risk-taking has been inhibited in a climate in which nothing can now be done by academics without reference to audit procedures of one sort or another. t is difficult to balance the costs and benefits of these changes. The unified UCAS system for undergraduate recruitment does seem to have reduced transaction costs in this huge internal market. The Research Assessment Exercise has plainly increased research outputs, especially in the new universities, though with the distortions of 'transfer markets' in researchers and with some probable displacement of quality and originality by quantity and routine.[2] The Teaching Quality Assessment system seems to have been introduced, however, without any built-in measures of its own consequences for standards, which may well have negative effects, through the displacement of effort, as well as positive ones. On the whole, it seems that the harmful effects of these systems have been mitigated by the extent to which academics have been able to keep control of them. Both the TQA and RAE systems are based on forms of peer-review, and have therefore been responsive to norms generated within the universities themselves. Professional autonomy has been less undermined in the universities than it has, for example, in the school system, or even in the NHS, where the 'internal market' now sometimes resembles a bizarre form of Stalinist planning in its rigidity and arbitrariness. What is even worse than not being able to treat patients because there are no resources, is not being allowed to treat them when there are resources, as does happen.

What has made the real difference, however, is that these changes have been introduced during a period when resources were being severely cut. In a pattern familiar across the rest of the public sector, the universities were made more accountable for 'standards', and to their 'customers', in a period when it was inevitable that standards would fall. It is not conceivable that standards of provision could *not* fall, when, according to Dearing, funding per student has declined by more than 40 per cent since 1976, and is scheduled to decline by a further 10 per cent by 1999-2000. [3]

---

2. The HEFCE's report of the 1986 Research Assessment Exercise described a significant increase in both the amount and assessed quality of research submitted.
3. The National Committee of Inquiry into Higher Education (Dearing Committee), 1997 (Main Report, p45).

I will explore further what I mean by 'standards' later on. But it is interesting to see how ideologically determined the whole system of quality audit has been. By focusing the inspection of quality on subject areas and departments in universities, and turning this assessment into a competition between them, a general interest has been created in demonstrating that standards have *not* fallen, or that if, by chance, they have, it is the fault of some guilty or hapless local providers, and not a general problem. The system has no mechanism for detecting declines in the quality of student experience of higher education even though 90 per cent of academics would probably agree that they have taken place, largely because of reduced resources. Of course, everyone can remember what happens to watchdogs which actually bark, such as HMI.

The Dearing Report

Here then was the context for the Dearing Committee's work. All political parties had acknowledged the existence of a serious funding crisis, within the constraints of taxation levels which the Conservative and Labour parties both accepted. All parties also agreed (in theory) upon the need to expand the number and proportion of students in higher education, from its present capped level of 30 per cent of 18 year olds, to something like 40 per cent over the next ten years or so. This was both for reasons of keeping up with other countries (a major theme of Dearing), and of ensuring that parental and student demand for university places, a main vehicle for upward social aspiration, was met. There was virtually-universal agreement across the university sector, new and old, that continued reductions in funding would threaten the fundamental integrity of the British higher education system. Vice-Chancellors said that if the present 'unit of resource' could be maintained, the present system may remain viable, but if it fell further, it would break. There was also a tacit and rather subtle consensus that the present system remained, in its essentials, a satisfactory design, and that the various reforms of the past decade, teaching and quality audits included, should stay.

There was thus a variety of demands that had to be reconciled in some fashion. Dearing, established on a bipartisan political basis, was nothing more than a device for reconciling them. Its chosen instrument, long signified in advance, was a form of hypothecated taxation, the 'graduate tax'.[4] Money could be found, expansion could be resumed, and the status quo of the university system continued for a further period of years, by this magic device. In the event, the new Labour government found it hardly necessary even to allow debate on the report, before adopting a version of its main recommendation which was more severe than Dearing's. Not only should students pay a flat rate contribution to tuition fees, the government said, but the student grant should be replaced by a loan repayable through the tax system.

Only the NUS, and a few Old Labourites, seemed to object. It might be politically impossible to increase income or wealth taxes, but there seemed to be no problem in redefining the income derived from 'graduate jobs' as a kind of windfall, 'deserving' repayment in the cause of justice to fellow-citizens who had not been given this earning opportunity. David Blunkett referred to cleaners who would otherwise be paying taxes to support the children of the privileged in universities, failing to observe that under a more progressive tax system her children might be benefitting from free higher education and she paying nothing.

Here then is an example of the surreptitious (or not so surreptitious) continuity between the post-Thatcherite and New Labour regimes. Dearing is a fitting monument to the managerial revolution in higher education. It has produced its predicted 'fix' (its members barely protesting when even this proved too fiscally demanding for the government), and has spent the rest of its hundreds of pages tinkering with the administration of the system that has evolved over the past two decades. As part of its proposed medium-term concordat between the university system and the state, Dearing accepts the need for some further centralisation of surveillance and control, via the proposed Quality Standards agency, pools of licensed external examiners, required teacher training for university lecturers and the like. (Note, however, that universal teacher training has not saved the schoolteachers from savaging.) The decline in innovativeness of a university system which has lost so much of its confidence and autonomy is reflected in the absence of challenging ideas or vision in this Report. The universities, like the rest of the public sector, are too weary and demoralised even to have noticed what is missing. A graduate tax

4. Geoff Mulgan and Robin Murray gave taxes on graduates' incomes as an example of 'functional hypothecation' in their 1993 Demos pamphlet *Reconnecting Taxation*.

may not be the ideal, but in these days who can quarrel with a lesser evil?

Radical choices for the British university system

Well, what broader dimensions of this problem should Dearing have taken note of? Where should a debate on the long-term future of the British higher education system start?

Perhaps what is most striking is the failure to make very much of the distinctive qualities of the British higher education system, in contrast to its comparators, though in fact a *sotto voce* view that it is *this* system that needs to be preserved pervades the Report and provides its implicit rationale. The virtues of the British system are quietly attested to in the Report's published annexes. Students, who were the subjects of a survey, profess high levels of satisfaction with their education, mitigated only by their concern at the lack of sufficient resources, books, small group teaching, and the like. Throughput rates (the proportion of students graduating in a three year period) are reported to be very high by comparison with most competitor countries (though there has been evidence elsewhere that wastage-rates have been rising). Staff are shown to be part of a remarkably uniform academic culture, in their commitment to teaching, scholarship and research, as all necessary elements of their professional role. Students, especially full-time students in the 'pre-1992 universities', value the opportunities for broad self-development which British university education, with its high proportion of students living away from home, and its rather generous infrastructure, provides.

Against this, the high-drop out, open-access, and low-contact higher education cultures of many other countries present a considerable contrast. One could regard our system, on this evidence, as a remarkable comparative national success. The question that one might ask about it is whether it could not become *more* of a national competitive resource than it already is, since it appears to offer a better educational experience than the higher education systems of many other advanced nations.

The question of whether the historically high investment in and intensivity of the British university system should be retained or dispensed with also needs now to be revisited in a radical way. The scale of investment in human capital is directly related to its outputs, including its marketable outputs. A large number of high-grade 'industries' in this country - for example, science, drama, medicine, the production of works of art and design, music - depend on the high-quality inputs and outputs of specialist university schools and departments. Without these, their vital reservoirs of new talent would soon dry up. The British economy should be in general becoming more skill- and knowledge-intensive. We should thus be looking to create more of these specialist centres of educational quality, not less. Britain happens, historically, to have a system which supports and sustains this quality, one whose 'traditional' virtues are (for once) advantages in 'modern' conditions. We should be seeking to maintain this as a source of comparative advantage, not diminish it.

I f one took the argument for creating a British higher education system of real excellence seriously, one would of course have to face up to a number of problems. It is clear that standards in the post-1992 universities and pre-1992 universities are not comparable, on many measures, including that of student satisfaction.[5] If there is to be a 'unified system', does it not have to become a more unified, and less stratified one, and the measures considered which might bring this about? It seems likely that the 40 per cent reduction in the unit of resource over twenty years has been damaging to standards. The reason is that education is so labour-intensive. It is not possible to economise on the quality and continuity of contact between students and teachers without impoverishing the learning process. It is not enough now merely to consolidate the present resourcing level, which is the best that the Dearing Committee seemed to believe was possible. It would certainly be helpful if alternative desirable unit levels of funding had been explicitly discussed, as the basis for considering different policy-options.

If the resourcing levels do not prove sufficient to maintain the high uniform standards that the Report advocates, it seems likely that pressures further to stratify and divide the system will re-emerge. Any further degradation of resource levels will provoke fresh demands from elite universities to be able to charge in fees what their markets will bear. A system offering broadly equal levels of provision to all qualified students will come at a high price, and there is little evidence that the government is willing to ask the populace to pay it.

---

5. Evidence of differences in the quality of experience of students and level of satisfaction from students in the old and new universities is given in the Dearing Committee's 'Report 2: Full and part-time students in higher education: their experiences and expectations'.

A worrying precedent for higher education is now being set in the secondary schools. Here the gap in achievement between private and state schools is growing. This is obviously the result of the huge resource discrepancies between them - in London some successful 'public' schools have five times the resources per pupil of state schools.[6] (This of course despite all the smokescreens of national curricula and standard assessments which are ostensibly intended to raise *all* standards.) With these visible differences in standards and outcomes, pressure for selectivity among state schools also grows. At this point we have a university system which is more universalistic, egalitarian, and fair, than the secondary system. (This despite the fact that half the Oxbridge entry comes from private education.) But not for long, if present trends continue, and as the differential aspirations nurtured by experience in the secondary schools impact on impoverished universities. Top-up fees and increasingly privatised elite universities cannot be long in coming if present trends continue.

A key issue which is only addressed in the weakest terms in the Dearing Report is that of equity between those who enter the higher education system and those who do not. This is the justification for the idea that graduates should be expected to pay back some of the additional earnings which have been made possible by their higher education. (Why, incidentally, is there no demand that employers should pay an additional tax on their graduate employees, since they are presumably also gaining added value as a result of the taxpayer's investment in them?) This is presented as an argument against a 'middle class welfare state', though needless to say the more logical remedy for this, a more progressive tax system, is deemed to be beyond the limits of debate.

What is also out of the frame of discussion is the idea that support for post-school education might be widened, removing the relative privilege of university entrants vis-a-vis those engaged in other forms of education and training. At an earlier stage it was argued by some that there should be a system of *comprehensive* support for post-18 education, to provide a learning entitlement which did not depend on academic qualification at A-level.[7] One advantage of

6. See the *Financial Times* annual schools survey for 1997, headed 'Independent schools take stranglehold', *FT*, October 11/12 1997.

a more universal system of educational support would be to encourage a greater diversity of provision, which could be more responsive to labour market needs than the present system. One gross distortion in higher education funding has certainly been its privileging of full-time undergraduate programmes over all others. There seem many advantages in giving transferable educational entitlements to students which they could then 'invest' in whatever programmes seem most beneficial them, and which are also able to meet appropriate requirements of quality. Such a system, if it were

'The more logical remedy - a more progressive tax system - is deemed beyond the limits of debate'

in place, could also support a reinvigorated adult education programme (one of the casualties of years of defunding), which would increase the diversity, and the available starting-points, of post-school educational opportunity for individuals of all ages. The Open University, one of the major achievements of the Wilson government, does not seem to have much of a place in the mind of new Labour.

Any extension of educational entitlements to young people presently excluded from them will involve an element of redistribution. To achieve this, funding might be provided for only two years of full-time equivalent post-school education, with student loans and/or tuition fees being required for any longer period. Such limits could meet the claims of justice between members of the same educational generation whilst still embodying the principle of one generation investing in the development of the next.

This practice of large-scale inter-generational transfers is perhaps one of the deepest structuring principles of the British system, though it is rarely recognised as such. The funding of the university system until now has been based on the assumption that education is an investment by the parental generation for the benefit of their children. The significance of a tax-based system, providing student fees and grants, is that the investment has been a collective one, by a generation of parents (and non-parents) for a whole generation of children. In paying taxes, one funded not only one's own children, but other people's, and tax-aversion, in this as in other domains, signifies

---

7. I published a version of this argument as 'Comprehensive Education after 18' in *For a Pluralist Socialism* (Verso, 1985). The idea had also been put forward by Oliver Fulton.

increasing unwillingness to do this.

Of course, no-one seriously imagines that the majority of students can in future pay the full costs of their higher education, with or without parental support. The development and occupational placement of their children will go on being a principal concern of most families. What will change under the new arrangements is that students must depend increasingly on their own families (and on their own mortgaged future earnings). And families, through the holding-down of tax levels, will have proportionately more resources to invest in their own children. The likely consequences of these changes for equal opportunities are quite obvious, as the privilege-offsetting qualities of the free tuition and means-tested grant system are weakened. Those whose families cannot or will not give support are weakened as a result. The families least able to give support, in emotional as well as material ways, will be those most battered by economic and social circumstances. Thus the higher education reforms of the new Labour government and the Dearing Committee make their own small contribution to possessive individualism, and to the idea that each generation must stand on its own feet.

The British system has historically been committed to a strong principle of 'social reproduction'. Originally, of course, this was an elite function, in which new generations were socialised into the norms and mores of the upper class through educational institutions (public schools, ancient universities, Inns of Court, etc.) which provided for intensive cultural transmission. Individuals selected on grounds of educational merit from lower social positions were strongly 'sponsored', as Ralph Turner's model put it, to ensure that they met the requirements of their new social location.[8] This originally aristocratic system was then extended in a meritocratic direction, to much of the middle class, (initially via grammar schools and redbrick universities), which retained the earlier model of strong socialisation and 'guaranteed' educational outcomes, though in a diluted form. In effect, a norm of familial transmission through the family was collectivised, and its functions transferred to other strong institutions. This origin is what has given the British higher education system its unusual cultural density. (This quality is usually

---

8. Ralph H. Turner, 'Modes of Social Ascent through Education', in A.H. Halsey, J.Floud & C.A. Anderson (eds), *Education, Economy and Society*, Free Press, 1961.

replicated in the elite but not in the 'mass' sectors of most other national systems, because of its functional value in reproducing educational quality.)

The issue now should be whether this model could now become a truly universalistic system, as additional populations gain access to it. The tacit assumptions of 'modernisation' seem to be that it can't, that the resources previously accorded for the development of 30 per cent of 18 year olds are unaffordable when we start to think of 40 per cent, 50 per cent or 60 per cent. Of course the rejection of this possibility, like the critique of middle-class over-use of the NHS, takes a deceptively pseudo-egalitarian form. Graduates must be made to feel guilty about receiving a free education, in order to legitimise the denial of this opportunity to others! But why should this future of funded, post-school education for all, be summarily rejected? At earlier stages, the aspirations to universal primary and secondary education were also considered to be utopian, but are now taken for granted. Why, in a 'knowledge-based society', should universal tertiary education seem so utopian? And why, at this stage, should the students be expected to pay for it themselves?

The rejection of this British model, which is probably what is taking place despite the universities' and the Dearing Committee's rearguard action on its behalf, will not take the form of its open repudiation. Equality of aspiration will be abandoned in the ostensible name of more opportunity, and not less. What will be constructed is a system which ostensibly offers more consumer choice, higher standards ('guaranteed' by audit), and greater flexibility. It will however be more competitive, provide less support, have higher rates of failure, and become more steeply stratified. It will become more of a mirror of the market society.

The softly-softly, consensual approach of Dearing is unlikely to be enough to defend the university system we still have, let alone the one we might like to have. If the system is to become more universalist in its scope, then the advocates of a more democratic university system need to become bolder and more visionary about it. If fragmentation and stratification through market forces is to avoided, then greater emphasis has to be placed on 'voice', on finding ways in which the various stakeholders in universities can make themselves heard.

Strong internal accountability, to students and staff, should be encouraged, even though to make this a reality requires resources. Students cannot be effectively empowered in universities without professional staffs to represent them with some continuity. Universities whose resources are often under-used for many weeks in each year, could make more of a contribution to local cultural and educational life than they do. Not only should universities be represented, as Dearing proposes, on the new regional authorities, but regional authorities should become important stakeholders in the universities themselves. If this leads to a greater diversification in the mission and character of different universities, so much the better.

Only if universities can demonstrate a commitment to being open, accountable and democratic institutions in the public domain, with a variety of forms of partnership with other institutions, will they succeed in making the claims on resources on the scale that they need. Holding actions are not enough. A democratic and universalist public sector will only survive in Britain if it finds some radical advocates who have not been cowed by the supposedly 'modernising', but actually marketising, revolution of the past two decades.

One explanation of the attrition to which higher education has been subject for twenty years is a self-fulfilling fear that more really must mean worse. This is the unspoken belief that needs to be challenged.

This article is also published in The New Higher Education: Issues and Directions for the Post-Dearing University, *edited by David Jary and Martin Parker, Staffordshire Unisversity Press, February 1998.*

Political science: a secret history
Paul Myerscough

Frederick Crews et al, *The Memory Wars: Freud's Legacy in Dispute*, Granta, £9.99

Prior to the publication of 'The Unknown Freud' in *The New York Review of Books* in 1993, Frederick Crews had received only as much - which is to say as little - attention as any English professor might expect during a career of inconspicuous modesty. 'The Unknown Freud', a survey of work reassessing psychoanalysis in the light of what Crews describes as 'surprising biographical revelations on the one hand and rigorous methodological critiques on the other', met with such a furious response in *The New York Review* that the exchange of letters had barely subsided before he was requested to write a new piece. This second essay, 'The Revenge of the Repressed', addressed the growing body of work assessing the phenomenon of 'recovered memory' or, as those authors favoured by Crews would have it, 'false memory'. The author's notoriety now established, the two essays and a selection of the correspondence which followed their publication have been collected together in *The Memory Wars*.

Crews is decided that the battle over the status of Freud's work must be fought on scientific grounds. Psychoanalysis, he insists, meets none of the criteria which would afford it consideration in 'scientifically serious circles'. A viable science produces hypotheses which can be tested, data which can be replicated, ideas which can be corroborated, and laws with predictive value. Psychoanalysis fails on all counts. It is a 'pseudoscience', whose concepts unsurprisingly find corroboration in clinical experience because those concepts are also the *a priori* assumptions of its interpretative framework. The 'self-authentication' of psychoanalysis is continually measured against the standards of an imagined laboratory, where fantasy has no place and dreams are interesting only in so far as their meanings can be verified through 'controlled research'.

Crews continues a line of attack on psychoanalysis whose most visible exponent has been Jeffrey Masson, former analyst and director of the Freud archives, who believes that in rejecting his analysands' accounts of childhood 'seduction' in favour of a theory of infantile sexuality, Freud succumbed to moral cowardice. Unlike Masson, however, Crews does not accept that the analysands' stories were their own to be accepted *or* rejected. Crews goes further, arguing that the stories were themselves Freud's invention, that his patients refused to accept his insistence on their lurid childhood experiences, and that, faced with an insupportable theory and increasingly disillusioned patients, he devised a new theory whereby, Crews asserts, 'it no longer mattered' what had happened to them as infants. This was the theory of repression, as applied to the constellation of fantasies later gathered under the rubric of the Oedipus complex.

Crews does not accept the existence of repression. Even if the concept were amenable to scientific assessment, he argues, such assessment would be redundant because experimental psychology has already demonstrated that memory is 'inherently sketchy, reconstructive, and unlocalizable'. It decays over time, is easily corrupted, and is most emphatically not to be conceived as an underground cavern, in which photographs of one's accumulated past are stacked in perpetuity, waiting to be unearthed should the therapeutic opportunity arise. In fact, the 'photographic' conception of memory described by Cruz is a million miles away from Freud's own. Fully cognisant of its mutability, Freud recognised the need to understand memory as a process of narrative reconstruction crucially bound up with the work of fantasy. But this is a reading one might obtain through a critical engagement with the span of Freud's work, its unending struggle to determine the possibility of separating truth from fiction, fantasy from real event. Crews is less synthetic in his approach, preferring selective quotation, the isolation of contradictions and the exposure of apparent falsifications in order to depict Freud as at best a shoddy scientist, at worst a charlatan and villain.

Barely restrained even in his quieter moments, Crews is unable to contain himself faced with the possibility of capturing 'Freud' in a metaphor. Thus he becomes a 'petty generalissimo' in his hold over fellow analysts and a 'pit bull' in his tenacious clinging to discredited ideas, whilst his true status should be recognised as that of King Lear, tottering abandoned on the heath, an Emperor parading without any clothes.

It is vital to Crews that this portrait convinces, for he wants to establish a philosophical and historical continuity between Freud's ideas and those underpinning the 'recovered memory movement'. It would be impossible, here, to convey an adequate sense of the antipathy Crews bears toward therapies based upon the 'restoration' of traumatic memories to paying clients presenting a myriad range of non-specific symptoms. Even at his mildest, on the second page of his introduction, we read that this 'frenzy...is now deluding countless patients (mostly women) into launching false charges of sexual abuse against their dumbfounded and mortified elders'. There is, he fulminates, a 'direct and dialectical' link between the 'dogma of repression' instituted by Freud, and the 'burgeoning plague' of recovered memory therapy besieging our civilisation.

And here we must pause, for it is as easy to mock Crews's rhetorical escalation as it is to submit to his relentless, wearying prose. No one disputes that if claims of childhood sexual abuse are the result of browbeating 'therapy' administered to vulnerable clients, then such malpractice should be exposed and made subject to legal censure. However, to blame psychoanalysis for the worst excesses performed in its name is a critical absurdity. Freud himself was careful to warn doctors against dabbling in 'wild psychoanalysis', and the crude model of memory retrieval attributed to recovered memory therapists is wilder than most.

If we are to understand Crews's insistence upon Freud's culpability for today's apparent injustices, then we must recognise that it is not only 'recovered memory' therapy, but therapy in general, which upsets him. This anxiety is reflected in his unquestioning assumption that science provides the means to dismiss Freud's 'demonology' for good.

Crews criticises psychoanalysis as a 'pseudoscience' on the basis that Freud himself insisted on the scientific credentials of his discipline. In fact, as John Forrester has shown in his recent *Dispatches from the Freud Wars : Psychoanalysis and its Passions*, Freud's claims in this respect were nothing if not ambiguous, couched in terms which problematise the received understanding of science as a positivistic approach to an objective set of phenomena. Psychoanalysis, argues Forrester, is a 'discipline of naturalistic observation and inference', closer in spirit to evolutionary biology or social anthropology than physics or chemistry. Moreover, since the knowledge produced by psychoanalysis is continuous with the domain of 'motives, intentions, reasons and beliefs' characteristic of everyday explanation, gossip, and the negotiation of human relationships, the empiricist ideal would require of scientific investigators of psychoanalysis that they take as their object the very phenomena against which science defines its notion of objectivity. Either they must 'lie down on the couch', in other words, or surrender the fantasy that a critique of psychoanalysis in the name of science could ever meet the requirements of a scientific enterprise.

In his response to 'The Unknown Freud', included in *The Memory Wars*, psychoanalyst David Olds describes analysis as 'a process of dealing with a wildly moving target from a slightly less wildly moving platform'. This image captures the unsettling indeterminacy which Crews finds so unbearable not only in psychoanalysis but, I would suggest, in interpretation generally. His horror at inconsistency is reserved not only for Freud's early speculations, or for the uncorroborated evidence of alleged victims' testimonies, but casts its shadow over the finest detail of his critique. Disagreement between analysts is a sign of 'disarray', a complex of evolving ideas becomes an 'utter conceptual murk', and fellow critics are evaluated strictly to the measure of their concordance with his analysis. In one extraordinary moment, Crews notes his regret that Elizabeth Loftus, a psychologist whom he otherwise admires for her stand against the 'myth of repression', was too slow-witted, in her expert testimony to the jury in a 'recovered memory' trial, to find the answers that Crews suggests would have disabled the prosecution utterly. What is revealed here is Crews's own fantasy of the perfect story, the interpretation which is beyond doubt, the evidence which renders a case irrefutable. Blinded by science, he cannot abandon the illusion of its purity, for it is the lack of such purity which he finds intolerable in the finally undetermined spaces of interpretation and human communication.

The struggle for power through the determination of meaning is, of course, a central concern in modern critical discourse, which maintains a tense engagement with certain versions of psychoanalysis. One would be hard-pressed, these days, to find a literary critic prepared to indulge a psychoanalytic reading of a text consisting in an excavation of the author's or characters' unconscious. One might, however, encounter a good deal of work historicising psychoanalysis as a 'symptomatic' late nineteenth century discourse, still more attempting to understand textual operations in relation to psychoanalytic concepts of meaning and narrative construction, and more still interrogating the limits and influence of psychoanalytic ideas in our understanding of a bewildering range of cultural phenomena.

It may or may not be surprising that Crews identified himself as a psychoanalytic literary critic at the beginning of his career in the 1960s. This, and his subsequent drift into disaffection with Freud's legacy, can now be charted as an historical progression towards his current position, but nothing in that history prepares us for the vituperativeness of the articles collected in *The Memory Wars*. If this is the rage of apostasy, then it does not stem from Crews having abandoned his faith in psychoanalysis only to embrace another in natural science. In the 1975 preface to *Out of My System*, a volume of essays which traces his growing ambivalence towards psychoanalysis, Crews is clear that his primary allegiance has always been to empiricism. He had come to sense the need to distinguish between '"scientific" and "ideological" strains of psychoanalytic thought'. Psychoanalysis, for Crews, had been the discursive reflection of his own struggle to mediate between 'empirical responsibility and urges toward deep and revolutionary explanation'. In *The Memory Wars* we witness the final triumph of a scientific rationalism in which revolutionary responsibility has been displaced by an urge toward empirical explanation.

I n his introduction to *The Memory Wars*, Crews accounts for his loss of faith as the result of his 'collision' with philosophies of science, a process of quiet but 'painful realization' achieved through scholarly reflection. Later, he dismisses as an 'echo of Dr Strangelove' one critic's suggestion that 'Freud-baiting' is best seen as a political activity, an attempt to 'define and manage' the culture's understanding of bodies and minds. In 1975, however, Crews recalled his turn away from Freud as a decision crucially bound up with politics, and specifically with a conflict of allegiance during the student uprisings of the late 1960s. His radicalism under pressure, the psychoanalysis with which Crews identified his revolutionary urges, became the casualty of his new-found loyalty to 'fragile and irreplaceable institutions'. In *The Memory Wars*, this suspicion of collective action finds its targets in feminism, which Crews sees as the ideological force propelling the recovered memory movement, and in a homogenised middle-American mass, 'a community steeped in Biblical literalism on the one hand and *Geraldo* on the other'. Whatever the force of Crews's argument in individual cases, its extension is driven by a deep fear of the group, of a feminism in which victimhood becomes the 'test of authentic belonging', and of a mass whose collective consciousness is rendered increasingly suggestible by a combination of regressive theology and the culture of confession. In defending against this perceived erosion of autonomy, Crews is fighting for 'fragile and irreplaceable' institutions once more, for a version of the truth founded in a more or less humanistic, more or less paternalistic scientific rationalism. It is a nostalgic picture of the world, one in which traumatic repression has no place, memory now subject to the gentle atrophy of forgetting, and in which families are freed from the threat of violence and desire. It is a world in which reason prevails, and psychoanalysis has nothing to offer. It is also a world in which refutation, Crews's last word in *The Memory Wars*, would be sufficient to vanquish the enemy for good. In his triumph, Crews might take a moment to ask himself, as Freud asks his own interlocutor in John Forrester's imagined dialogue with the resurrected analyst, why despite all his certainty, he still feels the need to demand 'truth of a dead man'.

A woman of substance
Joanna Clarke Jones

Claire Tomalin, *Jane Austen: A Life*, Viking, £20

In her new biography, Claire Tomalin aims to dispel two enduring myths about Jane Austen. First, that in the words of her older brother Henry: 'Hers was not by any means a life of event'. Second, the commonly held perception that she lived in the gentrified world portrayed in her novels. In fact, as Tomalin points out, Austen lived in a very different type of society - a meritocracy or 'pseudo gentry' - a changing Hampshire world of clergymen, lawyers and MPs, rather than the monied land-owning classes she wrote about so freely.

Jane Austen was born the seventh of eight children to a clergyman father in the country parish of Steventon. Money was a constant cause of concern to the Austens - all they had to live on was the meagre salary of George Austen. The struggle to survive financially was to be a theme of Jane's life. As a single woman who did not marry, she was dependent on the kindness of others (meaning men) for her security, until she started earning money from her books. As she warned her niece Fanny in a letter: 'Single women have a dreadful propensity for being poor.'

Austen did not leave a diary, and many of her letters were diligently destroyed by her sister Cassandra, wary of the too caustic comments about family and friends. Her brother Henry did the same, presumably anxious to keep up the edited, austere version of his sister he was at pains to convey. Nevertheless, and from the scant resources at her disposal, Claire Tomalin has created a fascinating study of Jane Austen and her world. She traces how the turbulent events of the outside world affected families such as the Austens, and influenced Jane in her writing.

People in the south of England were particularly affected by fear of the French terror spreading across the Channel. The Austens were no exception, with their constant fears about financial stability, a number of their family in the armed forces, and family connections with France, through the irascible cousin Eliza. Jane Austen has been criticised for her silence on matters political, and assumed to take on board Tory values. Tomalin shows that her writing contains hints of political and social insight. She draws a parallel in *Mansfield Park*, for example, between Britain under the morally bankrupt leadership of the Prince Regent, and the conflict between the principled Fanny Price and the pleasure-seeking socialites Henry and Mary Crawford, who do not care how their actions affect others.

While Jane herself was not of this social type, she attended her fair share of informal parties in her youth, and fell in love with an Irishman named Tom Lefroy, with whom she behaved quite outrageously, as she admits in one of her surviving letters to Cassandra. Both knew the match could never be, as neither had any money. Tomalin writes of this time in her life: 'it is the only surviving letter where Jane is clearly writing as the heroine of her own youthful story, living for herself the short period of power, excitement and adventure that might come to a young woman when she was thinking of choosing a husband; just for a brief time she is enacting instead of imagining.' Tom Lefroy is sent away, finds a new, more suitable wife, and Jane is left to rely on her imagination for romance and marriage, and a changing picture of her own life - settling into premature middle age with her sister, who was also disappointed in love when her fiancé died.

This is prefaced, however, by a long unhappy barren period, shiftless and travelling round the country with her parents, when she does not write a word for ten years, having written her first three books by the age of twenty. We are often led to wonder what would have happened if Jane Austen had given up her writing talent in favour of love and marriage, and the inevitable constant stream of ten or eleven babies, before dying in childbirth, as happened to a number of her sisters-in-law.

Austen is evidently glad to have avoided that fate. She later has the opportunity to marry Tom's brother, but gives up this last chance of married security in order to continue writing. We see her finally find peace in a new home in Chawton, where she prodigiously writes her last three books and finds a modest degree of fame and fortune as a writer before her mysterious illness and death. The most moving tribute to her life was written by her devoted sister, who said of her: 'She was the sun of my life, the gilder of every pleasure, the soother of every sorrow, I have not a thought concealed from her, and it is as if I had lost a part of myself.'

Claire Tomalin masterfully portrays a new Jane Austen - not a dry chronicler of a static world she knew well, but a vital woman, alive to the pleasures and disappointments of her own life, separate from the world of her imagination, so vivid and acute that people mistook what she wrote for autobiography. The book provides a compelling account of the life of a hugely talented woman, rooted in both political and social history, and the family's own circumstances. It is entertaining and highly readable, and the meticulous scholarship involved shines through every page.

A Fine Romance
Rebecca L. Walkowitz

Ian McEwan, *Enduring Love*, Cape, £15.99

If the house of fiction has many windows, it also has many curtains. Shades of partial revelation regularly ornament the late twentieth century novel. What adorns perspective also occludes it, and the curtains take as well as give. The visible frame of narrative draws our attention to its rhetoric, to the substance and the fact of the frame. While it may be tempting to associate this image of fictional viewpoint with the ever-popular 'unreliable narrator', the term underrates both the menace and the familiarity that attends these structures of address. Ian McEwan's every work elaborates this menace and makes fiction of this familiarity. His most recent novels relate allegories of reading as literal and uncanny experience, as the revived dead metaphors of everyday life.

McEwan's novels often seem to be about the condition of desired and failed delimitation, the sort of never-ending and imprecise proliferation of meaning that metaphor engenders. His latest novel, *Enduring Love*, leaves us to ponder the various conditions promised by its title: love that persists, the state of suffering such persistence, the kind of love that exists when one is suffering, persisting, abiding. His previous major work, *Black Dogs* (1992), offers up a cliched repertoire it will not reproduce, confronting and overcoming the banality of symbolism by presenting it, sometimes mocking it, at every turn. Thus a 'black dog' corresponds to high drama as well as low idiom: although it variously appears as a bout of depression, a dishonourable person, a symbol of evil in a nightmare, or an attack animal trained by Nazi soldiers, we find it also in more prosaic figures, as the proverbial 'patience of a dog' and a 'hot dog' bought in a city street. To the extent that McEwan allows his metaphor to register as both transcendent evil and take-away dinner, he dares us to consider the 'blasphemy' - an important word in both novels - of narrative: what happens when you make a rational story of visceral events, a singular account of 'universal' incident, whether the fall of the wall in Berlin or the experience of Nazi concentration camps in Poland.

Enduring Love moves away from these moments of global history, but is similarly structured by traumatic encounter and symbolic resonance, and by the opposition of scientific and humanistic explanation. The novel opens with the meticulous assembly of a primal scene, a picnic in the Chilterns abruptly interrupted by a ballooning accident in which Joe Rose and his wife Clarissa witness the gruesome death of a would-be rescuer. We are encouraged to see that the novel's beginning is 'a fall' in every sense. A man plunges to his death from a height of several hundred feet, threatening the pastoral romance of a couple named 'Rose,' a familiar symbol for Paradise, among other things. The scene introduces Jed Parry, who sees in the disaster a manifestation of divine knowledge, a knowledge of love he must share with Joe. The allusiveness of this 'fall' is not lost on Clarissa, a scholar of Romantic poetry, who invokes the Miltonic Lucifer as another angel thrust from 'th'Ethereal Sky'.

The novel is told in the first person by Joe, a science journalist and one-time physicist whose intent rationality is challenged by Jed's evangelical pursuit. Joe's narrative is disrupted from time to time by Jed's demanding, deluded love letters, which are given as separate chapters in the text.

Finally there are two 'Appendices' in the form of an article reprinted from a psychiatric journal and a last letter from Jed. The first documents a case of 'homo-erotic obsession, with religious overtones', the latter confides Jed's persistent faith that he has seen in the sun's rays Joe's acknowledgment of their love. Although the 'romance' between Joe and Jed and the marriage of Joe and Clarissa are the 'enduring loves' explicitly shown in the novel, there are several analogous relations we are meant to see: Jed's love of God, Joe's love of science, Clarissa's love for John Keats and her hunt for an elusive final letter to Fanny Brawne, the widow's love for her husband killed in the accident, Clarissa's love for children. McEwan's palimpsest revives an overworked symbolism by making its embarrassing exhaustion part of the story he tells. *Enduring Love* manages its weighty topics - 'love' and 'evil' - within a modern sensibility because it seems to recognise that irony has become itself an easy expectation, a tired trope of self-conscious narrative.

Rather than wit, then, McEwan's style more nearly approaches 'blasphemy', menace, sacred topics just slightly out of place. As Jed's fervent adoration is a 'syndrome' rather than, say, an insight, it is a profanity both of religion and of love. Joe understands it as 'a dark, distorting mirror that reflected and parodied a brighter world of lovers whose reckless abandon to their cause was sane'. He likes to imagine that he can know the distinction between sanity and distortion, sacred and profane, but Joe's rationalizing manias are a proximate alternative to Jed's aggressive actions. Blasphemy turns out to offer its own parables, lessons about its own interpretation.

Jed is the figure of radical perspective come to life as character in the novel. His experience corresponds to Joe's metaphors: where Joe remembers that he and Jed rushed 'towards each other like lovers' as they converged upon the faltering balloon, Jed imagines he is a lover. Joe's simile is Jed's reality. For Jed, the marginalia of interaction become the content of a message: he is certain, for instance, that the very literal curtains along Joe's windows convey and strategically obscure a love he cannot otherwise express. Watching Joe's apartment from the street below, Jed writes to say he 'got it straight away... I feel it too.' Jed's interpretations - the meaning of 'the accident', what 'happens' in his first encounter with Joe, the intention of Joe's casual brush against a shrub, the 'real' love behind Joe's articulated rejections - are most menacing because so insistent. By their extremity, they exhibit the presumptive assurance of Joe's readings, and ours. Indeed, the curtains that ornament this novel, as so much of McEwan's elegant work, show us the windows that limit and facilitate our fictions.

Race, space and the postmodern subject
Reina Lewis

Avtar Brah, *Cartographies of diaspora: contesting identies*, Routledge, £14.99 pb, £47.50 hb

Avtar Brah's contributions to discussions of 'race' and gender will be well-known to many. This book offers a clear and broad-ranging collection of her work in the field over the past two decades. Some of the chapters will be familiar to readers from their initial publication in journals and books since the early 1980s. Brah's range is vast, from social science interview methodologies to the latest in political theory and cultural criticism. All is handled with an even-handedness that will explain, to readers new to her various fields, the historical and material circumstances in which the ideas in circulation today emerged. Readers familiar with these developments will on this account forgive the book its occasional repetitions. Brah's keen exposition of contemporary political, cultural and social theory never fails to offer a provocative evaluation that takes us through the older material towards her central arguments and provides a welcome opportunity to rethink existing protocols in the light of new ideas.

Central to all her work is an insistence that the discourses which racialise do so in relation to other differentiations of class, gender, sexuality, religion, region, generation and so on. Brah uses a variety of examples to demonstrate how racialising powers and institutions work performatively and contingently, producing multiple subject positions whose particular sets of contradictions can be traced to their moment and trajectory of coming into being. She is interested not only in how racist discourse overcomes the evident contradictions of its peculiar logic (the tiny number of immigrants that Thatcher held were swamping 'British' culture), but also in the potential of congruent and conflicting identifications to be politically mobilising and progressive. It is in this context that she offers the concept of 'diaspora space' - as a site in which the confluences between the different diasporas found in contemporary societies can produce 'differential racialisations'. This concept aims to avoid the simple binarisms of a minoritising discourse that presents both minority and majority as homogeneous and hermeneutically sealed oppositions.

By seeing diaspora within a 'multi-axial performative understanding of power', one can recognise that a group constituted as a minority 'along one dimension of difference' may be constituted as a majority along another. For example, an Asian woman who is constituted as the minority subject of an 'ethnic minority' may , within a discourse of caste, be constituted as a majority subject, superior to others. Brah's approach also allows for the recognition of intra-diasporic relations, those between India and Africa that precede British colonialism, for example, or between Afro-Caribbean and Irish diasporas. Such recognition, in its turn, can decentre the Eurocentrism of much minoritising discourse.

It is Brah's hope that the concept of 'diaspora space' can 'place discourse of home and dispersion in creative tension, inscribing a homing desire while simultaneously criticising discourses of fixed origins'. This is not to say that diaspora ideologies do not often centre on precisely the demand for a homeland and the reification of 'tradition'. What Brah offers is a way of seizing the concept of 'diaspora' and reconfiguring it, wresting it away from conservative tendencies while acknowledging the social, psychic and cultural desires that drive fantasies of belonging. To this end Brah distinguishes 'diaspora space' from the concept of diaspora, with its implicit emphasis on return.

Brah interweaves 'genealogies of dispersion with those of staying put' in order to speak about the 'here and now' of people's lived realities of multiple and differential racialisations. This allows the diaspora to be inhabited not only by those seen as newly arrived, but also by those seen as apparently indigenous. Reformulating the popular concept of border crossing, as metaphor and actuality for a postmodern condition, Brah speaks of diaspora space as the point of congruence of various forms of dis/location. Diaspora space is the intersectionality where 'multiple subject positions are juxtaposed, contested, proclaimed or disavowed', a space that cannot but invoke borders and their transgression. This diasporic space produces new subjectivities about which Brah is hopeful, just as she is hopeful for a form of 'theoretical creolisation' that, like diaspora, takes ideas from different places in order to address the contradictory subjectivities and positions which the late twentieth century creates.

Brah is keen throughout that theoretical concepts should be enabling and not lend themselves to 'hegemonic cooptation' by the forces they seek to challenge. This politicised motivation means that her intellectually stellar analysis of concepts such as essentialism, ethnicity, and culture and lived experience, reconnects them to the materiality of labour conditions, and the organisation of sexuality and of social spaces from which they are sometimes woefully detached. This approach is particularly welcome when Brah considers debates about modernity and postmodernity in relation to the presence, or often absence, of the 'non-West'. Her challenges to essentialism and insistence on seeing culture and identity as ever-changing processes also means that her overview of multi-cultural and anti-racist politics in Britain (and to a lesser extent the USA) is nuanced and constructive.

Diasporic space is a concept that shifts away from the closures and ranked hierarchies associated with the worst aspects of identity politics. That it allows for individual experience and collective organisation, without diminishing the multiple and contradictory differentials that divide at the same time as they unite, is very appealing. Brah's foray into autobiography in sections of the book serves not only to demonstrate the contradictions of the speaking/ writing subject, but also to keep reminding the reader of the materiality of racialising and other differentiating discourses, as they are experienced.

Active Welfare

Across the great divide

Welfare and culture in Britain and Europe

The creation of a 'modern' welfare state is a central plank of new Labour's programme. But what does this mean for the consumers of welfare and those who in different ways depend on personal and community social services? What models of the lived experience of welfare are informing policy? Government rhetoric often seems to be an uneasy alliance of borrowed ideas, some with their origins in Europe and some in the USA. But how much do we in Britain really know of the cultures of welfare of our closest neighbours? The articles in this special issue draw on the experiences of practitioners in several European countries and provide a unique insight into the different cultural and political bases of state-citizen relationships which construct and are constructed by 'active welfare'. One particular theme is how racial and cultural differences are variously understood and negotiated within different national contexts. Another concerns the articulation between local possibilities and globalised trends in immigration and the displacement of populations. Comparative welfare in the English speaking world has found it hard to cross the divide of language, and learn from the grassroots experience of continental Europe. This themed section of Soundings challenges us to cross the divide, and learn from the creativity of users and practitioners.

Europe or America?

One night in 1986 I gathered with a group of friends to mark the departure of one of our number to live in the USA. The Westland helicopter affair was unfolding, and sometime late in the evening we all fell into furious argument about this. The row seemed to spoil and distract from what should have been an occasion for sadness and well-wishing. Only next morning did it occur to me that it had all been a displacement; just as it seemed that Thatcher's government might be torn apart by a dispute over a small and inconsequential aerospace company, so I and my group were unable to handle our conflicting feelings about the loss of a friend to the States. The symbolic link between the two, which allowed the former to serve as the vehicle for the latter, revolved around the question 'Do we belong with Europe or America?' At root the Westland affair turned on which of the two great blocks of capital Britain would be primarily allied with in the coming years. Maastricht and EMU notwithstanding, this question still haunts whole spheres of British public and political life.

A superficial analysis of new Labour's language of welfare discloses a profound continuing ambivalence about this question, as well as a worrying tendency for indiscriminate borrowing in pursuit of a new 'vision'. The story quoted at the begining of John Pitts' article in this issue, of how Jack Straw came to incorporate 'Yankee curfews for kiddies' into his juvenile justice reforms, may or may not be apocryphal, but it captures well the sense of randomness which pervades current welfare policy formation - a (French) Foyer here, a dash of (American) communitarianism there, some (Euro) anti-social exclusion measures, a dollop of (American) welfare to work, and a Scandinavian-style modernised monarchy to round matters off. Some might argue that this simply reflects the impact of globalisation on another domain of social life, but deeper analysis reveals a more complex situation, and profound questions about what kind of political choices are possible in a turbulent and protean political environment. 'Modernisation' is a key aspect of new Labour rhetoric, and the 1997 manifesto itself is replete with references to the desire to create 'a modern welfare state'. But what does modern signify in this context? In what way, for example, are the experiences of those who receive or participate in the consumption of welfare specifically modern? I want to find a way into answering these questions, partly by examining the origins of the collection of essays itself.

Welfare and culture

All the papers in this special issue were originally presented during an Economic and Social Research Council (ESRC) funded seminar series entitled *Welfare and Culture in Europe.* This project emerged at a particular point in the history of the study of modern welfare. Comparative welfare has a respectable history at least as long as the welfare state itself, but in the British tradition has suffered from the same constraints as the study and theorisation of welfare 'at home'. In its early days social policy in this country was strongly identified with the new discipline of social administration, which in turn was the academic breeding ground of the new class of welfare professionals, especially social workers, who were to be the engine of reforming welfare within the Beveridge vision. The corporatist and technocratic assumptions implied in this vision of welfare and social work were challenged first by Marxist and then by feminist analyses. Political and theoretical debate thus came to revolve largely around questions of the nature of state formations and their relationship to the sphere of domestic and family life. In these configurations the idea of welfare as an autonomous or semi-autonoumous sphere of social life was largely subordinated to controversy over the production and reproduction of macro level relations of power. Feminist influences notwithstanding, within social work in the 1970s and 80s it was extremely difficult to make meaningful connections between the 'personal and the political', and the profession polarised sharply in a sterile and destructive antagonism between (supposed) political radicals and (supposed) reactionary psychoanalytic caseworkers. The category of 'culture' played little or no part in these debates, and where it did, it was in terms usually derided by the left, such as Keith Joseph's 'culture of deprivation' initiative.

Comparative welfare more or less reproduced the terms of these arguments, focusing its attention on the possibilities for reform and redistribution of wealth afforded by different models of capitalist social democratic welfare states. Many factors eventually converged to open up the 'new comparative welfare' which is still taking shape. Britain's definite, if ambivalent, move towards fuller integration into the EU under the Tories finally confronted us with the inevitability of a relationship with the continent founded on something more than weekend and summer tourism. Paradoxically, social anxieties about loss of sovereignty whipped up by the last Government have obliged national consciousness to wrestle with questions about what it might mean to be 'different' but 'integrated'. Although comparative welfare study had looked to the alternatives provided by some European models, particularly in Scandinavia, the focus was patchy and inconsistent. Occasionally news of some exciting and innovative reform would capture sufficient attention to open up more sustained enquiry - psychiatric reform in Italy and the Confidential Doctor Service experiments in Holland and Flanders are examples which come to mind. But systematic research or exchange of understanding about practice and grassroots organisation remained rare, and with hindsight it is possible to see that we continued to treat these instances as foreign exotica, and thus in principle incapable of being incorporated into our own thinking about ourselves. In turn we can recognise how the circulation of ideas, research and practices within the Anglophone world persisted as our primary comparative currency. North America and the Antipodes formed the other two points in a triangle of highly selective internationalism. Lastly, the dissolution of traditional academic boundaries in the social sciences, the emergence of new inter-disciplinary paradigms, and growing confidence in the validity of qualitative methodologies for researching social life, intersecting with the emergence of 'culture' and cultural studies as recognised sites of study also liberated us to think 'differently' about welfare.

Difference and reflexivity - comparing welfare practices

These were some of the stimuli which several years ago impelled two of the editors of this issue to become involved in comparative study of European child protection practices. Using small groups of practitioners in different countries, questionnaire responses to a single case study, and video recorded group discussions which we dubbed into the other language, exchanged and then asked the groups to comment upon, we found it possible to develop rich and 'thickly textured' comparative data which revealed the culturally embedded nature of professional thinking and behaviour. Linking these findings to analyses of the structure and ideological underpinnings of the socio-legal systems within which practices occurred, we were able to make preliminary comparative interpretations of the interplay between the micro, meso and macro levels of activity and reproduction in a particular domain of social life within a number of European nation states.[1] Several points about this methodology are relevant to the group of essays which follow.

---

1. A. Cooper *et al*, *Positive Child Protection: a view from abroad*, 1995; R. Hetherington *et al*, *Protecting Children: messages from Europe*, Russell House Publishing 1997.

First, we found that the reciprocal encounter with *difference* on the part both of the professional research groups and ourselves as researchers, resulted in a process not just of discovery but also of change. As we and they observed and recorded reactions of surprise, puzzlement, interest and suspicion in the

'The state is understood as less monolithic, more permeable to internal influences'

face of unfamiliar ways of thinking and acting, this led to an interrogation of the assumptions informing the practical world view of the 'other', but also of the 'self'. For participants in each country, looking as it were into a mirror in which they did not see themselves reflected back, a process occurred of disinterring the hidden

presuppositions informing their own practices as they struggled to understand those supporting the practices of their foreign colleagues. This *reflexivity* or enhanced capacity to stand outside ourselves and relativise our way of thinking and being by reference to the 'different other' is disruptive, disturbing and a potential source either of creativity or defensive retrenchment. On the creative side an opportunity is made for systematic self-critique, a chance to see old problems in new ways, and revise the categories of thinking which construct our social world, using models derived from the alternatives to which we have been exposed. The capacity to tolerate this disruption of the taken-for-granted is the precondition for allowing the 'foreign' and 'exotic' to be welcomed and incorporated. Equally, because such experiences are a challenge to 'tradition', they may evoke a fundamentalist reaction wherein, as Anthony Giddens has observed, tradition is defended in the traditional way.[2] In our comparative work the encounter with cultural difference, and the unexpectedly difficult and open-ended task of making sense of individual social and professional practices by reference to history, politics and ideology, meant that we came to see ourselves as more like traditional anthropologists than modern social scientists. *Anthropology as cultural critique* became the centre of the project.

Viewed like this, European comparative welfare both derives from and contributes to globalisation, disrupting the certainties of 'culture' as the 'way we do things here', even as it reveals these to us. By focusing on the lived experience of welfare practice, the contested and shifting character of social

---

2. A. Giddens, *Beyond Left and Right*, Polity 1994.

relationships, the 'politics of the vernacular' as John Pitts names it, these essays help transcend the traditional 'agency-structure' dichotomy in our theorisation of social welfare. As Stuart Hall observed recently, 'You can no longer think primarily in terms of the economic and the material and then add the cultural icing afterwards. You have to treat culture as formative of human life, human agency and of historical process...Political processes are often underpinned by deeper cultural shifts'.[3] It is not that 'the state' has disappeared from this analysis, simply that its constitution is understood as less monolithic, more permeable to internal influences, more a site and product of everyday struggle.

For the British reader, the authors' point of departure in some of these essays will seem fairly familiar, and in others rather less so. Either way, one could be dissuaded from persisting with the piece; but we think all of them contain surprises, unexpected shifts of perspective which disrupt our more settled ways of thinking about the politics of welfare. As I suggest above, this mirrors the experience of undertaking comparative study where the aim is to achieve some degree of qualitative depth.

Looking for the crevices

Hassan Ezzedine and Alain Grevot's account of a superficially uncontroversial project aimed at helping immigrant and minority ethnic children with educational difficulties describes how the traditional French school was conceived as a 'fortress' charged with the explicit task of instilling secular Republican values in children, whatever their provenance. The French politics of *intégration*, in which minorities have been effectively required to subordinate their cultural differences in exchange for full citizenship, is now experiencing severe strain. The young Muslim women who have in recent years challenged the secular principles of the education system by wearing headscarves to school, form the backdrop to the tensions at the heart of the project described here, in which the particularities of genuine 'need' clash and grind with the universalism and paternalism of the state formation through which welfare assistance can be provided. Their essay, like most in this collection, demonstrates the essentially *negotiative* character of welfare practice and welfare politics. Local conditions - and the lived experience of welfare is always local - are

---

3.   S. Hall & M. Jacques, 'Cultural revolutions', *New Statesman*, 5.12.97.

always complex but never fully determined. Helen Morgan's essay 'Looking for the Crevices' continues this theme, as she explores the new possibilities for alliances within the quasi-market of English community mental health work. As she says, 'Our central question was whether we could perceive cracks in the system as it changed that could be exploited to allow a more radical form of relationship between those who work in a service and those who use it.' She and her colleagues were invited by the purchasers of mental health services to intervene and build a partnership with users to establish some genuine authority for their 'consumer' voice. She deftly explains the central contradiction of the idea of a welfare market, but also shows how, with the right alliances, political and ethical space for progressive practice can be opened up. 'Purchasing departments, often staffed by people with little direct experience of mental health work, struggle to meet requirements from Government, whilst uncertain about what it is they are trying to do. The fundamental contradiction is that...they are not the ones who will use what they buy and are usually separated from those who will. We have a split customer.'

This view of welfare practice as occupying the 'contradictory spaces' within the welfare state formation has something in common with the movement, influential in the late 1970s and early 1980s, and sometimes glorified with the title 'possibilitarianism', which advocated activity 'In and against the state'. It also seems to me to differ on several counts. Not the least of these is a positive, unambivalent commitment to the principle of state or state-funded provision. Few left inclined welfare practitioners any longer harbour illusions about the obedient withering away of social distress and mental pain in the population once 'the state' has been persuaded to do its withering. The accounts in this collection are alive with the sentience of human predicaments, the anxiety, struggle and realism of those who suffer and work to alleviate suffering. The attention is more on how to maximise potential and reconcile contradictions, how to irk and irritate the system into a more responsive, humane and decent awareness of the predicament of people trying to live ordinary lives. 'We may be ill but we're not stupid', say the users in Helen Morgan's account.

Welfare culture and state formation

The perspectives adopted in this approach to 'user empowerment' hold out some hope of achieving a settlement between the right to citizenship and the fact of mental or emotional disturbance which has often been taken as a disqualification of the former. The Italian mental health reform movement of the 1970s resolved this tension by opting firmly for a political rather than a radical therapeutic solution to the problem of the incarceration and social marginalisation of the psychiatric population. Today, in those regions of Italy where the spirit of the reforms lives on, this ideology remains strong. Manifestations of psychiatric disturbance in public places are responded to as a public order problem, not a mental health one as in Britain, in order not to place the individuals concerned outside the frameworks of ordinary citizenship. The contrasting fates of the British and Italian mental health movements of thirty years ago are instructive. The former was characterised by profound 'anti-statism', therapeutic radicalism, and not a little ideological romanticism. It spawned some of the most creative and influential of psychiatric thinkers in recent decades, and some daring experiments in therapeutic community living. But today its tangible legacy is minimal, surviving only in the shape of a few small organisations, such as The Arbours and the Philadelphia Association, committed to exploring the boundary between psychoanalytic and political concepts of therapeutic living. The Italian experiment by contrast remains a potent force at the heart of the welfare state, still drawing legitimacy from the original Law 180 which required the closure of the old hospitals and the establishment of alternative community-based provision. Yet there is a suspicion that these achievements have been at the expense of an engagement with subjectivity and the irreducible 'interiority' of mental distress.

Nevertheless, in Margherita Gobbi, Angelo Cassin and Monica Savio's account of a training initiative for community psychiatric nurses, psychological symbolic 'homelessness' is presented as the key metaphor which articulates the fear of the consequences of mental ill health. As they observe, neither hospitals nor community care can create a real home, the lifelong network of emotional, personal and social bonds which stable affective relationships bring. It may be that the Italian ideal to 'replace the full time protection of the asylum's walls with the symbolic walls of social integration', is more realisable than we would think in Britain, because many communities themselves remain more 'integrated' than here and hence more willing and better equipped to manage the vicissitudes of psychiatric disturbance in their midst. In Britain there has been an idealisation of the caring potential of 'the community' as something new, to replace the 'old' psychiatric bins; in turn the place of the asylum or hospital in the total scheme of care has become denigrated. As the authors point out, the fear of 'homelessness' in Britain articulates not an anxiety about the social isolation of those who endure mental health problems, but the host community's *fear* of the mentally disturbed among them; this is one reason why the community transpires to be a less welcoming and caring place than we have liked to imagine. But, arguably, this fear also speaks to something real. Perhaps neither country's policies have really taken on board the extraordinary psychological demands involved for those who are in close daily contact with psychotic disturbance. The psychoanalyst Donald Winnicott quoted a colleague as saying 'Mental illness consists in not being able to find anyone who can stand to be with you', and this may be the truest expression of psychological homelessness.

> 'The French, positive, concept of political freedom differs from the negative British model of "freedom from" state interference'

John Pitts' comparative study of the social and political context of responses to youth crime on the Dickens and Flaubert housing estates in East London and the Parisian suburbs respectively, is also a powerful reminder of the differing trajectories of the state tradition in France and England in recent decades, and the significance of this for local welfare activity. He shows that the success of French national social crime prevention initiatives was rooted in the strength of local networks of community and political organisation, which were able to give meaning and structural continuity to the resources made available by the Mitterrand administration. At a deep level, the French state is founded on the assumption of a social contract with the people, and, in return for their obeisance to the Republican ideal the contract means that the state is expected to sustain and promote their inclusion, their capacity for participation in civic and political life. The concept of political freedoms in this paradigm is positive, rather than the negative one inscribed in the British model of 'freedom from' state interference. As John Pitts argues, Thatcher's attack on the institutions of local government and the network of intermediate structures of civic society renders the aspiration to promote social cohesion in the new ghettoes of British society extraordinarily difficult. The series of 'projects' which constitutes the effort at social crime prevention on the Dickens estate can find no coherent local political structure in which to take root.

'You are in Africa now' shout the Maghrebian children of the Flaubert estate when the English party arrives for their visit. In reality some of the neighbourhoods described in these papers are global villages; in Beauvais, Hassan Ezzedine's project works with families from at least 7 countries; over 100 languages are spoken in Tensta, the Stockholm suburb which is the site of Livstycket, the employment project for ethnic minority women discussed in Angela Leopold's paper. She draws out particularly well the multiple possibilities and dilemmas of welfare work with minority groups situated within the shifting ideologies of the host nation state; and how the latter may put the former to work in the service of providing reassurance and solidity for the frailty of its own sense of 'cultural identity'. Tensions surrounding gender relations in a project which empowers women personally and economically are an additional dimension in the complex process of change which is the history of Livstycket. Yet the beauty of her account lies in the sense that a 'negotiative politics' is possible if the realities of people's cultural inheritance and their potential for creativity is respected and nurtured, not controlled and managed. Each moment of progress brings in its train a new contradiction, challenge or question. An authentically dialectical stance towards social reality requires a capacity to respond to uncertainty, to grasp the shape of the emergent trends without limiting the contribution of human agency. Marx and Engel's famous dictum probably applies across all dimensions of social life - we make our own histories but not under conditions of our own choosing.

Transformations of welfare

The women of Tensta have exploited 'the market' and succeeded in putting their own distinctive stamp on the local economy. Yet, reading about Livstycket, one is struck by how the project recalls a much earlier, pre-capitalist, artisanal mode of socio-economic organisation, in which the link between personal or cultural creativity and economic production is not broken. The idea of non-alienated labour has been important to welfare based employment schemes in continental Europe, which has often been less tentative than we have in Britain about 'reinserting' economically excluded people into the economy, because they have found ways to achieve this on terms not entirely dictated by the exigencies of commodity production. I once visited a community psychiatric day centre in

Italy, in a city which had been at the forefront of the reform movement. The psychiatrist there explained that when the old hospital closed down they had wanted to smash the looms on which patients had been obliged to work during their incarceration. But, thinking again, they preserved them, took them to the new centre and established a workers' co-operative producing woven goods. The looms, he said, were a reminder of their suffering, and of the work of transformation which is the object of both mental and manual labour.

This is as good an image as any to represent the idea of 'active welfare'. It speaks to the need for some kind of reciprocity between those who in Blair's new 'giving society' will be doing the giving, and those doing the 'receiving', between the old and the new, and the old and the young. Without this, the project of 'modernisation' in welfare will simply succeed in producing new and probably more insidious forms of exclusion.

AC

Dickens and Flaubert

A tale of two housing estates

John Pitts

*John Pitts contrasts Mitterrand's innovative policies
on young people and crime with the approach of
new Labour.*

In June last year the *Observer* was compiling a feature on the zero tolerance
in the United States of anyone deemed anti-social. I phoned Jack Straw,
then the Opposition's home affairs spokesman, and asked if he would be
following the Americans' hard line. 'Now Jack', I said, with that slightly
hysterical laugh it is always wise to use when addressing the New Labour
leadership, 'You won't be introducing Yankee curfews on kiddies out after
bedtime will you?'

My certainty was misplaced. Straw, thinking off the top of his head,
decided child curfews were a splendid idea. Once he began considering
their charms there was no stopping him. 'There are a lot of complaints
about youngsters out on the streets until late at night,' he said. 'I see
them when I'm driving back from the Commons and wonder where their
parents are.'

I put the phone down and went to tell the editor we had a story. An
hour later, Straw called back. He didn't mean what he had said, he implied,
and had not been authorised to make an announcement. Would I pull the

article? Journalism's machismo culture demands that you always reject politicians' attempts to tell you what to write. And I did, reasonably and politely.

But machismo can often lead to ruin and the curfews case was no exception. Because we printed the story, New Labour decided they would look weak if they did not clamp down on tots. The party's intellectuals considered curfews with a solemn respect for the integrity of public policy and cobbled together a curfew package on the back of a fag packet. If I had not run the article, it would not have happened. I'm very sorry.

Nick Cohen, *Observer*, 28 September 1997

NEW LABOUR AND LAW AND ORDER

In the run-up to the 1997 general election, there was considerable speculation on the left about whether new Labour's apparent 'toughness' on crime was simply a way of stealing the issue of 'law and order' from the Conservatives. Indeed many who are politically and professionally involved in youth justice believed, and continue to believe, that behind the electoral window dressing is a government which will be both more compassionate and more intelligent in its dealings with children and young people in trouble with the law. Thus, they predict that the hard-hitting Crime and Public Order Bill, due in late 1997, will be softened significantly in its passage through parliament, and that an urban policy, which gets to grips with the social origins of crime in the poorest neighbourhoods, will be the centrepiece of Blair's second term.

However, this optimistic view ignores the centrality of 'law & order' to Labour's electoral strategy and its political fortunes. The issue of youth crime offers the example *par excellence* of the lessons Labour election strategists have learnt from the electoral successes of Ronald Reagan, Margaret Thatcher and Bill Clinton, and the popular success of Michael Howard. For each of them, 'law & order' in general, and the implicit promise to contain the threat posed by non-white young people from the 'ghetto' to those in the economic mainstream, was an electoral hermetic which served to solidify an otherwise socially disparate political constituency. It is also a strategy which aims to heal rifts within the party, promising to be 'tough' enough 'on crime' for the modernisers and 'tough' enough on the 'causes of crime' for old Labour's remaining 'social engineers'. But 'Tough on Crime ...' is no mere expendable electoral cliché. On 4 September 1997, addressing social service managers and professionals at a conference on new directions in social welfare, Norman Warner, Jack Straw's adviser on youth justice, stated that controlling youth crime remained one of the Government's top priorities and that its resolve would be evident in the Crime and Public Order Bill (1997). This message was reiterated by the Home Office minister Alan Michaels at the *Crime Concern* AGM on 10 September. It is possible, of course, that Warner and Michaels have forgotten that Labour won the election on 1 May and are mistakenly continuing to churn out the soundbites. It is far more likely, however, that they mean what they are saying.

Like Clinton's new Democrats, new Labour believes that to gain and hold political power they have to win the suburbs. If 'Worcester Woman' is to change her voting habits permanently, new Labour strategists reason, she must be made to feel that the government will contain the threat posed to her property, person and peace of mind, not to mention the educational opportunities of her children, by the roughly spoken, badly behaved young people who haunt the streets of the inner city and the estates on its periphery.

There is, however, more in play here than the crude manipulation of the anxieties of potential voters. New Labour's stance on young offenders, and its conflation of bad behaviour and crime, derives from an intellectual orthodoxy which appears to have united politically active intellectuals of all complexions. On the right is Norman Dennis who traces a clear line from welfare dependency, via excessive sexual intercourse, to youth crime and public disorder. Slightly further to the right, Charles Murray, ably assisted by Andrew Neil and the *Sunday Times*, pursues the link between welfare dependency, premature and profligate pregnancy, and crime, while offering spurious quasi-scientific 'proofs' that the increased use of imprisonment would significantly reduce the crime rate. Approaching things from a different angle, from what is often referred to as the 'post-Marxist left', Beatrix Campbell points to the crisis of post-industrial masculinity, coupled with police passivity, as the motor of the barbaric behaviour of young men on council estates. Back towards what, in the late 1990s, constitutes the political centre, the journalist and social commentator Melanie Phillips, writing in *The Observer*, traces contemporary problems of crime and social disorder to the introduction of 'progressive' educational methods and the simultaneous emergence of moral relativism. She urges teachers to return to traditional classroom techniques, and parents to specify clear moral values which accord with those of the right thinking majority. Whatever else may divide them, most of these pundits are agreed upon the need for more state control of the bad behaviour of the young and their feckless fathers, and less state support for their welfare dependent mothers. These ideas find their most coherent expression in the highly influential version of 'communitarianism' offered by Etzioni, a doctrine which has been cited approvingly by both Tony Blair and Jack Straw. Etzioni writes:

> Communitarians call to restore civic virtues, for people to live up to their responsibilities and not merely focus on their entitlements, and to shore up the moral foundations of society.
>
> *The Spirit of Community*, p ix

He speaks of a pressing need to address the collapse of a common moral base and to inject a moral dimension into the task of social reconstruction. For Etzioni, the public humiliation of wrongdoers, 'naming and shaming', serves 'to underscore society's disapproval of the crime', ... 'temporarily marking out those convicted in open court, after due process, seems a legitimate community-building device'. He indicates that the 'community' must act as 'a reinforcer of pro-social mores', and that in this endeavour there is little room for tolerance of minor infringements of rules, laws or norms, or minor acts of public disorder.

New Labour's commitment to these ideas was signalled in *The Blair Revolution*, by Messrs. Mandelson & Liddle:

> Schools require a new, much tougher, set of disciplinary sanctions to deal with unruly and uncooperative pupils - such as compulsory homework on school premises, weekend and Saturday night detention, and the banning of favourite leisure pursuits such as football matches.
>
> This greater emphasis on discipline should be matched in the local community. The police, schools and local authority services must work together closely to crack down on vandalism and other antisocial behaviour. Excessive tolerance of low-level sub-criminal behaviour by unruly young people undermines general respect for the rule of law, ruins the environment and makes a misery of the lives of many innocent people - and

provides a breeding ground for more serious crime.[1]

A problem with this uncritical absorption of US-style electoral strategy and social philosophy is that ministers now appear to believe that we really are facing American-style crime problems. Thus, Jack Straw fulminates against 'aggressive beggars', human windscreen wipers, and the unaccompanied ten year olds who hang around the chip shop in Kentish Town High Street after dark, as if he was talking about Chicago's South Side Ghetto where firearms-related homicides, rather than mumbled requests for 'spare change', are an everyday reality.

Hard Labour

Ultimately, new Labour's analysis of the problem of youth crime reduces it to a simple by-product of the moral failure of families, the cupidity of young offenders and the stupidity or incompetence of the professionals who are supposed to contain and educate them. As a result, the two-pronged strategy of punishment and prevention they have devised to combat youth crime is not particularly subtle either.

Punishment

The Crime and Public Order Bill (1997) will propose that youth courts have the power to 'name and shame' young offenders. It will introduce Parenting Orders requiring the parents of young offenders to participate in parental re-education programmes and Child Safety Orders (curfews), for children aged 10-17, which may be enforced by the use of electronic tagging. The Bill will introduce an Action Plan Order which will require young people to pursue an intensive three month programme specified by the court, sometimes involving their parents. It will also introduce a Reparation Order, of between one and three months duration, which will require youngsters to confront their victims and 'work off' their 'debt to society', possibly through some form of labour. The government also proposes to transfer 18 year olds to the adult courts and to remove responsibility for young offenders from local authority social services

---

1. P. Mandelson & P. Liddle, *The Blair Revolution*, Faber 1996.

departments and relocate it with a 'toughened' Probation Service. These changes will further blur the distinction between the youth and adult courts, while eroding the legal rights of the children and young people who appear in them. Although Jack Straw will be ending Michael Howard's ill-starred 'boot camps', it is likely that the number of places in Secure Training Centres for the custodial confinement of children of twelve and over will be increased.

'Jack Straw recently stated that prisons are a demand-led service'

The changes which are likely to have the greatest impact upon the numbers of children and young people sent into custody are the replacement of repeat cautioning by the police with a final warning, and the repeal of the conditional discharge. The final warning will be given to a child or young person when they enter the youth justice system for the second time. Should they offend subsequently they will proceed directly to court, where their case will be tried by a stipendiary magistrate. At present most police divisions in the UK operate a 'Caution Plus' programme which offers repeat offenders further cautions if they agree to engage in specially designed programmes or undertake certain educational or social activities. These young people will now proceed directly to the youth court where the conditional discharge currently used in around 28 per cent of cases, has been deleted from the options available to the bench.

Asked recently how he planned to respond to the growing prison population (between 1992 and 1995 the number of juveniles aged 15-18 sentenced to custody rose from 3,900 to 5,100) the Home Secretary, Jack Straw, answered that prisons were a 'demand-led service' and that if the bench chose to impose custodial sentences it was his job to provide the cells.

Prevention

Both Norman Warner and Alan Michaels have described new Labour's youth crime strategy as long-term. By this, they appear to be suggesting that, over the long term, the impact of *prevention* will obviate the need for *punishment*. The renewed enthusiasm for 'prevention' in youth justice in England and Wales grew out of a disillusionment with the apparent inability of the youth justice strategies of the 1980s to contain or reduce youth crime. The Conservative government's blood-curdling rhetoric notwithstanding, youth justice in the 1980s was primarily concerned with the cost-effective management of the youth justice system. This led to a unique and ironic situation in which the most vociferous 'law and order' government of the post-war period found itself presiding over unprecedented reductions in the numbers of young people consigned to custody. This occurred, moreover, in a period in which the crime rate soared to record heights.[2]

Economic stringency and the dominance of individualistic explanations of youth crime dictate that, unlike the 'preventive' initiatives of the 1960s and 1970s, which often sought to effect political and social change, 'prevention' in the 1990s will only 'target' problematic young people, their families and their schools. In 1995 the UK Audit Commission study of the operation of the youth justice system in England and Wales concluded that resources could be better spent on prevention. In so saying, the report identified as the keys to effective youth crime reduction assistance with parenting skills, structured pre-school education for children at risk, support for teachers dealing with badly behaved pupils and the development of positive leisure opportunities for crime-prone children and young people. The report was welcomed by the Labour Party which indicated that its recommendations complemented its own youth justice strategy.

These measures are to be complemented by an education, training and US-style 'welfare to work' initiative which will offer young people who would otherwise be excluded from participation in economic life, a stake in conformity. This marks a somewhat grudging acceptance of a link between unemployment and crime, and indicates a belief that employment will offer such a stake. However, the recent bungled attempt to encourage the young, and overwhelmingly under-qualified, unemployed to take up surplus university places suggests that this part of the strategy is, to say the least, at an early stage in its development.

Regrettably, both the analysis of the problem of youth crime and new Labour's strategy for tackling it, duck the most important questions. Namely, what has happened to youth crime in Britain since 1979? What do these developments tell us about the direction in which our society is moving, and how might we change direction?

---

2. J. Pitts, 'The Politics and Practice of Youth Justice', in E. Mclauglin and J. Muncie (eds), *Controlling Crime*, Sage Publications/Open University Press 1996.

A redistribution of crime and wealth

Between 1981 and 1991 the number of workers earning half the national average wage or less, the Council of Europe poverty line, rose from 900,000 to 2,400,000. In the same period those earning over twice the national average rose from 1,800,000 to 3,100,000. At the same time, recorded crime in the UK increased by 111 per cent. Between 1981 and 1995 crime rose further and faster in the UK than in any other western European country.

Although, in the 1980s, official statistics showed a steady reduction in the numbers of young people involved in crime, statistics published in 1992 indicated that while the *numbers* of 10-17 year olds convicted or cautioned by the police had fallen by around 25 per cent between 1981 and 1991 (the 1980s witnessed a 25 per cent drop in the numbers of 10-17 year olds in the population) *recorded offences* committed by children and young people had risen by 54 per cent over the period.[3] An analysis of British Crime Survey data for the period 1981 to 1991 went some way to explaining this bald statistic. Not only did it reveal a substantial increase in the volume of crime and victimisation in the preceding decade, it also indicated marked changes in its nature and geographical distribution.[4] Taken together these data indicated both an intensification and concentration of youth crime in the UK in the 1980s.

The British Crime Surveys reveal an alarming picture. They divide neighbourhoods into ten categories on the basis of the intensity of the criminal victimisation of their residents. By 1991, the chances of a resident in the lowest crime neighbourhood ever being assaulted had fallen to a point where it was barely measurable. Residents in the highest crime neighbourhoods, by contrast, now risked being assaulted twice a year. This polarisation of risk is made clearer when we recognise that, by 1992, residents in the highest crime neighbourhoods experienced twice the rate of property crime and four times the rate of personal crime than those in the next worst category. These findings point to a dramatic redistribution of victimisation towards the poorest and most vulnerable residents over the intervening ten years.

---

3. A. Hagell & T. Newburn, *Persistent Young Offenders*, Policy Studies Institute 1994.
4. T. Hope, 'Inequality and the Future of Community Crime Prevention', in S. P. Lab, *Crime Prevention at a Crossroads*, American Academy of Criminal Justice 1995.

As the 1980s progressed, a combination of the government's 'right to buy' policy, the curtailment of the right of local authorities to spend housing revenue on house building, and progressive reductions in central government's financial contribution to local government, ensured that less and less public housing stock was available for rent. These developments presaged significant demographic changes in which relatively prosperous older and higher income families left housing estates in the inner city or on its periphery, to be replaced by poorer, younger families. As a result, whereas at the beginning of the 1980s the average council house tenant's income was 73 per cent of the national average, by the beginning of the 1990s it had fallen to 48 per cent.

'People were disconnected from each other and participation in local political and social life fell away'

By 1995, over 50 per cent of council households had no breadwinner. The estates which experienced the greatest changes saw increasing concentrations of children, teenagers, young single adults and young single parent families. These neighbourhoods also became a last resort for residents who had previously been homeless, hospitalised or imprisoned, and for refugees from political persecution.

These rapid demographic changes quickly eroded relationships of kinship and friendship, transforming these estates into aggregates of strangers, who were often deeply suspicious of one another. This had a number of consequences.

These changes meant that those people most vulnerable to criminal victimisation - young single parents, Black and Asian families and the single elderly - and those most likely to victimise them - adolescent boys and young men - were progressively thrown together on the poorest housing estates. In their study of one such neighbourhood in the early 1990s, Tim Hope and Janet Foster found that a 40 per cent turnover in population over three years was paralleled by a 50 per cent rise in burglaries. However, rapid population change meant that traditional forms of informal social control also disappeared.

Alongside the disappearance of informal systems of social control we saw the erosion of traditional systems of informal social support for parents, young people and children, which often make the difference between whether a child or young person can be sustained in a fragile or volatile home or not. The American criminologist Elliott Currie writes:

Communities suffering from these compounded stresses begin to exhibit the
phenomenon some researchers call 'drain': as the ability of families to support
themselves and care for their children drops below a certain critical point,
they can no longer sustain those informal networks of social support and help
that can otherwise be a buffer against the impact of the economic grinding of
the market.

Because people were disconnected from one another, participation in local
political and social life fell away, and so people had no basis upon which to join
together to exert political pressure, bid for resources and make demands on the
local and central government agencies with responsibility for the problems they
confronted.

High crime neighbourhoods tend to be highly concentrated and have a
distinctive economic structure. In Britain in the 1980s, neighbourhood
destabilisation, by eroding economic links between poor
neighbourhoods and their local economies, reproduced this structure in growing
numbers of poor neighbourhoods. In the proces, inner city retail, industrial and
commercial concerns, which had once been central to the social and
demographic stability of working-class neighbourhoods, either went out of
business or relocated in the industrial and retail parks on the periphery of the
city. The impact of this mass evacuation was compounded by a policy shift in
the mid-1980s which meant that training resources followed employers rather
than 'job-seekers'.

The crime and violence in these neighbourhoods is implosive in that it is
committed by, and against, local residents. This intra-neighbourhood crime
pattern is a distinguishing characteristic of high crime areas in Britain. Their
other distinguishing feature is that the young people involved in this crime,
being denied the means to make the social transition to adult roles and
responsibilities, do not 'grow out of crime'. It is against the backdrop of this
expanding pool of economically marginal, reluctant adolescents that the
intensification of crime and public disorder in the poorest neighbourhoods in
Britain must be understood.

The capacity of schools in these areas to resist neighbourhood
tendencies towards lawlessness has been progressively undermined by the
knock-on effects of neighbourhood destabilisation. In the north London

school where our current research is based, the transience of the neighbouring estate is reflected in a 50 per cent turnover in the school roll between years 7 and 11 (ages 11-16). Because the nature of the changes in the neighbourhood has been to replace more prosperous residents with less prosperous ones, by 1997 over 50 per cent of school students qualified for free school meals. The school has twice as many students with serious behavioural problems as neighbouring schools and, last year, 30 per cent of the staff left.

In *Learning From Failure*, a study undertaken by the Centre for Educational Management at the Roehampton Institute, researchers analysed 15 schools designated by OFSTED as failing. The study found that 'failing schools are serving communities with high levels of deprivation, unemployment, single parent families and high uptake of free school meals'. This is particularly ironic when we remember that the Government, Home Office researchers and professionals in the community safety industry all locate the school as the institution *par excellence*, in which the struggle against youth crime will be conducted.

The plight of the families in these neighbourhoods has been compounded by cutbacks in local government expenditure, which have resulted in the withdrawal of many of the educational, youth service, community development and social welfare services which had previously contributed to the quality of communal life and social cohesion in their neighbourhoods. However, it is not simply that there was greater need and fewer organisations and individuals available to respond to that need. In the 1980s, the nature of both public services and 'publics' themselves has changed. The 1980s witnessed swingeing cuts in local authority budgets, a substantial redistribution of political power from local to central government and the parallel introduction of 'market forces' into public services. In this period, decisions about the goals to which public services should strive, their spending priorities, and the day to day conduct of their staff were increasingly taken by central government, or the government's appointees in the burgeoning, and largely unaccountable, quangocracy which progressively annexed public services in the 1980s. Together, these forces have seriously restricted the capacity of local agencies to make a concerted collaborative response to the profound problems experienced by the residents of destabilised neighbourhoods.

A TALE OF TWO HOUSING ESTATES

Between 1993 and 1995 my colleague Philip Smith and I were involved in a
study of the responses of public professionals, politicians and local residents
to youth crime and the violent victimisation of children and young people on
the Dickens Estate in East London and the Flaubert Estate in an industrial
suburb to the West of Paris.[5] In many ways, the two estates typified the
changing pattern of crime and victimisation on socially deprived public housing
estates in the two countries.

The struggle for 'space' and the struggle for 'inclusion'

A key difference between the Flaubert and Dickens estates is that, like other
poor French suburbs, the area, the geographical space occupied by the Flaubert
estate, is not the object of contention between different racial or cultural groups.
On our arrival in the suburb the young people shouted 'you are in Africa now',
suggesting what was for us a very unfamiliar separateness. In France, African
and Mahgrebian people are likely to live on relatively remote, geographically
demarcated, largely non-white, estates on the periphery of towns and cities - a
spatial pattern more akin to the USA than Britain. The white residents of the
old town, it seems, have no desire to reclaim the estate, while the families of
the white residents on the estate arrived at around the same time as people of
other races and appear to feel no special racial or cultural affinity with it. Young
people in the French suburb, black and white, feel 'excluded' rather than
'embattled', their geographical remoteness serving as an apt metaphor for the
social distance which they see as existing between them and those who hold
political and social power . The struggle for these young people has concerned
what they perceive to be an oppressive educational system which denies them
opportunity, and an oppressive state which has sometimes responded to their
protests with brutality.

On the Dickens estate the struggle for space and the defence of territory is
central to the violent conflict in the neighbourhood. The key issue in the

5. J. J. Pearce, 'French Lessons: Young People Comparative research and Community
    Safety', in *Social work in Europe* Vol.1 No. 33, 32-36; and J. Pitts, 'Public Issues and
    Private Troubles: A Tale of Two Cities', in *Social Work in Europe*, Vol.2 No. 1, 3-11.

successful British National Party campaign of 1993 concerned whether or not local space was to be occupied by 'local' people. Inter-racial conflict was evident throughout the research period, and local young people, educational, youth justice and welfare professionals all attributed this to the desire on the part of some white residents and their children to defend 'their' school and 'their' neighbourhood against an influx of Bengali school students and homeless Bengali families into what had been, up to that point, a largely 'white' neighbourhood.

During our research, violence in general and racially-motivated violence in particular on the Dickens estate reached record levels, making it the most violent neighbourhood in a traditionally high-crime London borough. The Flaubert estate, having topped the French youth crime league in the early 1980s, now had a level of crime and violence somewhat below the national average. The Flaubert estate had been the focus of the Social Prevention Initiative (SPI) launched by Francoise Mitterrand in the early 1980s.

The French Social Prevention Initiative

Upon its election in 1981, the socialist administration of Francoise Mitterrand faced nation-wide riots in the multi-racial *banlieus* (suburbs). Fearing that they might reach the proportions they had attained in Britain, Mitterrand established the *étés jeunes*, a 100,000-strong national summer playscheme, and a commission of town mayors under the chairmanship of Henri Bonnemaison. The Bonnemaison commission was concerned with both the prevention of crime and those forms of 'social exclusion' which appeared to threaten social cohesion. Thus, in its report, the Commission argued that if youth crime and disorder in the *banlieus* were to be curbed, the solution must lie in a process of political incorporation, an expression of solidarity with the people who lived there. Although evaluation has been uneven, the SPI undoubtedly made a significant impact upon youth crime in France. In 1981 in both Britain and France, approximately 3,500,000 offences were recorded by the police. By the end of the 1980s, the number of offences recorded in Britain was approaching 6,000,000. Meanwhile in France, between 1983 and 1986 there was a decline in recorded offences to around 3,000,000, from which the figure rose gradually to around 3.8 million by the end of the decade. In France, the fall in crime was most marked in those categories of offences most frequently committed by children and young people.[6] Moreover, whereas in Britain in the 1980s crime rose fastest in the poorest neighbourhoods, in France it was in the poorest neighbourhoods that the fall in crime was most marked. This fall in crime was paralleled by the abolition of the death penalty in 1981 and a reduction in the prison population, by means of an amnesty, in the first three months of Mitterrand's premiership from 42,000 to 30,000. Further measures of 'grace' and amnesty were extended to French prisoners in 1988 and 1989.

In her evaluation of the impact of SPI, De Liege points to the importance of its political and administrative structure in the realisation of its goals.[7] The National Council for the Prevention of Delinquency, chaired by the Prime Minister, and attended by the majority of town mayors and senior civil servants from the ministries of Justice, Housing, Education, Health and Social Affairs, was established in June 1983. The Council determined the relationship which should exist between central and local government, the structure of inter-professional and inter-agency co-operation at local level, the roles to be played by public professionals, the resources to be devoted to the discharge of these roles, and the space for negotiation between elected officials, administrators and citizen groups. At Regional level, Councils for the Prevention of Crime, chaired by the chief civil servant (the *Commissaire de la Republique*), with the Chief Judicial Officer (the *Procureur de la Republique*) as the vice-chair, were established. At local level Communal Councils for the Prevention of Crime, chaired by the town mayors, were created. Communal Councils monitored local youth crime patterns, established special working groups to deal with particular problems and targeted central government funds on these problems. In his evaluation of European youth crime prevention initiatives John Graham notes that:

> The main aim of the Communal Council is to reduce crime through
> improving the urban environment, reducing unemployment among the young,
> improving facilities for education and training, combating racial
> discrimination and encouraging the assimilation and integration of

6. M. King, 'How to Make Social Crime Prevention Work, the French Experience', NACRO 1988.
7. M.P. De Liege, 'Social Development and the Prevention of Crime in France: a Challenge for Local Parties and Central Government', in M. Farrell and F. Heidensohn, *Crime in Europe*, Routledge 1991.

marginalised groups, particularly alienated youngsters and immigrants. To facilitate this process, a national network of Youth Centres, known as *Missions Locales* has been set up in more than 100 towns and cities. These centres try to bridge the transition between school and work for the unemployed and the unqualified (aged 16-25) by offering youth training and advice and assistance on matters such as improving literacy, managing financial affairs and finding accommodation. They also encourage young people, particularly the unemployed, to set up and run their own projects.[8]

Social Prevention on the Flaubert estate

On the Flaubert estate local employment policy aimed to offer local jobs on the estate to local people in order to reduce local unemployment and reinforce community ties. A national youth and adult training agency, *Association Jeunesse, Culture, Loisirs, Technique* (JCLT), was contracted by the *Mairie* and the *Mission Locale* to offer youth and adult training and social and cultural activities on the estate. Professionals recognised that racism and the poor reputation of the estate often made it difficult to place people in employment beyond the estate but their emphasis on extended periods of training leading to nationally recognised qualifications meant that they had achieved some success in equipping residents for skilled, higher-paid, jobs in primary sector employment in the *Département* and in Paris.

This policy was devised by the Town Council, the *Mission Locale* and the *Conseil de Quartier* elected by local residents aged 16+. Local housing policy was developed in a similar way. It pursues social stability via a strategy of locating relatives of different generations in proximity to one another. The pursuit of this policy has, amongst other things, led to the construction of new, larger, low-rise flats on the Flaubert estate. This is of particular interest when we note that the key issue in local elections amongst some white residents of the Dickens estate and its environs concerned housing. Beyond the ideology, in east London, as elsewhere, council house sales and a freeze on council housing revenues have generated a genuine shortage of accommodation which has served to exacerbate racial tensions in the area.

---

8. J. Graham, 'Crime Prevention Policies in Europe', in *European Journal of Crime, Criminal Law and Criminal Justice*, Vol. 1 No. 2.

In addition to the relatively formal *Conseil de Quartier* on the Flaubert estate, there was a women's organisation, the *Femmes Relais*, which was a network of Senegalese, North African, Kurdish, Iranian and Portuguese mothers, supported by *animateurs sociales* (community workers) from the mayor's office, who met regularly with representatives of the schools, the police, the local administration and relevant welfare agencies, to discuss problems affecting their children and devise new policies and strategies.

T he other meeting point between the politicians and the people on the Flaubert estate was *La Pagode*, a centre constructed by the Mayor's Office where young people met *animateurs sociales* to undertake the recreational, educational and political activities in which they were interested. Over the three years it has been in existence, the 500 or so users have produced a regular newsletter, *Alors... Quel de Neuf* , which discusses issues affecting the estate and the young people on it. About sixty young people attend monthly meetings at *La Pagode* with the mayor or his deputy, at which these issues are discussed and policy options are considered.

It is evident from our study that the developments on the Flaubert estate flowed from the political possibilities created by the policies of *Decentralisation, Deconcentration, Social Prevention* and the *Politique de la Ville* introduced by the Mitterrand administration in the 1980s. By allowing space for political innovation at a local level, they created the ground for a localised 'Nouvelle Democratie'. This local political participation connected, via the town's Mayor, to the Crime Prevention committee chaired by the Prime Minister of France of which all town mayors were members. This made it possible, at least, to influence the priorities of local officials and of central government departments, as well as the manner in which these departments cooperated at local level, and the ways in which their resources were deployed; there was an attempt to realise shared goals which were, in part at least, formulated in consultation with local citizens. It was also possible to institutionalise this activity, politically, administratively and professionally, at national, regional and local levels and, apparently, to do so without too much bureaucratic stultification. This is a politically driven system, with a range of political, administrative, and professional feedback loops which

'Allowing space for political innovation at a local level created the ground for a localised "Nouvelle Democratie"'

ensure that there is a strong connection between policy, provision, professional practice and the needs, interests and wishes of the intended beneficiaries.

These structures have been central to the realisation of the developments on the Flaubert estate, but so too has been the congruence between the political values of the citizens and professionals engaged in them, and those articulated within French social policy. It has been noted that the vocabulary of Mitterrand's *Politique de la Ville* was derived in large part from the French social work profession, whose numbers were increased, and whose professional status and political influence was enhanced significantly, by the crucial role played in the realisation of the *Politique de la Ville*.

Crime prevention on the Dickens estate

David Downes has observed that employment schemes on the Dickens estate have, for their duration, been effective in diverting young people from crime, or minimising their involvement in it but, when these schemes terminate, their impact is quickly dissipated.[9] This points up two key differences between the Dickens estate and the Flaubert estate. Crime prevention on the Dickens estate has traditionally taken the form of time-limited projects, emanating from beyond the estate and unintegrated with the activities of the established local and central government and voluntary agencies operating there. Not only were they unintegrated at agency level, they rarely articulated with the plans and strategies of the local administration. Patterns of funding, which increasingly promoted an arbitrary opportunism amongst local agencies and local politicians, dictated that those projects which were realised tended to come with fully-formed and non-negotiable 'targets', and unrealistic 'exit strategies', which required the under-funded local authority to make unrealistic commitments to future spending. This process has led to considerable cynicism amongst both professional and local residents about the viability of developing a safer neighbourhood on a project-by-project basis; a feeling articulated most clearly by research participants who visited the Flaubert estate in Paris.

All this stands in marked contrast with the, sometimes open, hostility with which social workers and other public professionals in Britain were regarded by

---

9.   D. Downes, 'Public Violence on Two Estates', Home Office 1990 (unpublished).

central government in the 1980s. Research shows that social workers were concerned about the falling standard of the service they were able to provide but sceptical about the efficacy of grassroots or local political pressure to effect change upon those factors which generated the problems encountered by the children and young people for whom they were attempting to provide a service. They appeared to have reconciled themselves to narrowing their professional focus, and the redefinition of their task as the efficient exercise of the statutory functions of their agencies, no more, no less.

This inevitably meant that their scope for innovation and responsiveness to the 'public' was restricted. Asked to describe what role the local authority social services department might play vis-à-vis the high level of assaults on Bengali school children, two senior officers of the authority observed, ironically, that, at best, the victim might be made the subject of a child protection investigation and the perpetrators, if they were ever apprehended, could be required to pursue a correctional programme at the Youth Justice Centre.

Bureaucratic and resource pressures meant that a decision to co-operate with other agencies or professionals was often determined by whether, and to what extent, such co-operation would enable public professionals to discharge, or indeed displace completely, their primary tasks. Of all the agencies contacted during the research, only the police could anticipate a crime prevention initiative which did not take the form of a new 'project' funded from elsewhere, which would involve the development of new agency imperatives rather than the manipulation of existing ones.

London respondents did not perceive any positive local or central government political leadership behind the changes they experienced, and their actions were shaped, defensively, by the attempt to avoid attracting sanctions from local politicians if the agency 'fell down on the job' (i.e. failed to discharge its statutory responsibilities adequately). This anxiety was heightened during the research when a new administration with a mandate to centralise previously localised services was elected, raising the spectre of demotions and redundancies.

Political engagement

The conflict on both the Flaubert and the Dickens estates is profoundly political. However, whereas on the Flaubert estate there has been a sustained, and fairly successful, attempt to engage young people in new forms of political participation and, through this, to enable them to articulate their demands in the national political process, on the Dickens estate the gap between the vernacular politics of the locality and the formal structures of local and national politics is vast. This is, in part, a product of the erosion of the power of local government by central government in the UK in the 1980s. The National Front was able to achieve the daunting power and influence it did in East London in the early 1990s because it exploited local discontent about housing. It is at least arguable that had the local authority been able to use its housing revenue to build new homes, or indeed, to purchase 'hard-to-sell' properties in nearby Docklands, the National Front would have made little headway in the area. This would also have gone some way to assuaging the fears of local people that a council which had once been attuned to the needs and wishes of local people had been replaced by a bunch of 'do-gooders'.

In the 1970s and 1980s many white residents on the Dickens estate came to believe that they, along with other white working-class people, had been abandoned by the Labour Party. For some this perceived betrayal left them feeling beleaguered. They felt that in their area, the birthplace of London socialism, the local Labour Party, having originally gained its power and its political mandate from people like them, had now switched sides.[10] The old-style political organisation, headed and sustained by local people, and characterised by a multiplicity of personalised, formal and informal face-to-face relationships between party members, local MPs, councillors and trades unionists, was central to the social and economic organisation of the area. But the decline of the docks triggered the dissolution of the complex forms of social organisation associated with the white docklands community. Meanwhile the Bengali community was developing its own forms of social organisation, creating a stratified micro-society with its own legitimate opportunity structures and its own politics. For white working-class residents, however, nothing had come to replace the old forms of social solidarity.

On the Dickens estate today there is very little on offer to white young people in the political supermarket. It is either the 'Front' or the 'antiracism' and anti-sexism they learn in school. However some white young men, and not a few white young women, view such 'anti-oppressive' politics as a bizarre attempt

10. P. Cohen, *Island Stories: Real and Imagined Communities in the East End*, Runnymede Trust 1995.

to characterise them, and their families, as culprits rather than victims, who have been left to fight a hopeless rearguard action in defence of an identity, a territory and a way of life, which is under siege. As a result, 'anti-racist' and 'anti-sexist' initiatives in education, the youth service and welfare agencies often inadvertently compound the problems they strive to solve.

Perhaps one of the most remarkable contrasts between the Dickens estate and the Flaubert estate concerns the degree of political engagement between young people, local politicians and professionals and the congruence between their political objectives. On the Flaubert estate this engagement has been achieved by an administrative and political structure devised in consultation with all of the potential 'stakeholders'. As a result, neighbourhood conflict between young people, adult residents, professionals, the police, children's judges and politicians can be handled in face-to-face encounters between the protagonists. On the Dickens estate, by contrast, there is virtually no contact between young people and local councillors. Some Bengali young people are members of national and international Islamic political and religious youth organisations, but most white young people remain politically disconnected. Meanwhile, in the Town Hall, new and old Labour jockey for control of the key committees.

The politics of solidarity

Not since the American Poverty Programme of the 1960s has there been a governmental assault upon the problems of youth crime and social cohesion on the scale of the French Social Prevention initiative of the 1980s and 1990s. However, the French initiative emerged from a different political tradition, adopted a radically different political strategy and, in consequence, had a different effect upon the relationship between those on the social margins and the state. At the core of the political culture of both the USA and the UK is a notion of the state as a potentially antagonistic force which, unless it is rigorously controlled, may at any moment encroach upon the lives and arrogate the liberties of citizens. Thus 'freedom' consists in minimising the role of the state. In France, and many other Western European states, by contrast, the state is conceived as a potentially creative force, constituted by, and representative of, the collective interest of its citizens. Although both of these views are idealisations, they open doors to quite different political possibilities for governments trying to fashion

---

responses to the problems of crime and social cohesion.

Rather than circumventing the state apparatus, the task defined by Mitterrand and Bonnemaison concerned the construction, and then the institutionalisation, of a new relationship between the political centre and the social margins. This was to be achieved through the reform and co-ordination of the relevant ministries and a devolution of state power which aimed to repoliticise, democratise and localise key areas of state activity, and transform the practices of their agents. In consequence, for a time, the French initiative achieved the prize which had eluded the Kennedy-Johnson administrations, the construction of a political 'hotline' between the head of state and the ghetto.

The French initiative was born of a recognition that economic globalisation and a burgeoning new technology had transformed class relations, and that now, the key social division was between a contracting, relatively prosperous and skilled workforce and the growing body of, usually young and often non-white, people who appeared to be permanently excluded from economic activity altogether. This analysis marked an early recognition of the forces which were transforming advanced industrial societies throughout Europe and beyond. Its unique contribution was to devise new forms of social solidarity, and new routes to citizenship, to replace traditional but defunct, social and political structures rooted in the work place.

Should new Labour wish to achieve a more just and harmonious society or, indeed, if it simply wished to reduce youth crime, what, practically, might it do? It would probably strive to offer a stake in society to those who have none through the repoliticisation of local government and the development of educational and vocational opportunity in the poorest neighbourhoods. It would therefore have a direct interest in the simultaneous revitalisation of 'communities' and local economies in order to put an end to the chronic waste of human lives which structural youth unemployment represents, and to reduce the burgeoning costs of the crime and disorder it generates. If new Labour really wanted to do this, then the French Social Prevention Initiative suggests some intriguing possibilities; but, perhaps more importantly, it poses some crucially important questions about the basis of citizenship, participative democracy and social relations in a post-Fordist society. To date, however, these are questions which few British politicians have had the nerve to ask.

Livstycket

Working with immigrant women in a Stockholm suburb

Angela Leopold

Angela Leopold *describes a project for ethnic minority women in Stockholm.*

Livstycket means 'corset'. The word consists of two parts: liv ('waist') and *stycke* ('piece'). But *liv* also means 'life', so the name of the project, *Livstycket*, suggests both a snug support and a Piece of Life. Livstycket includes about sixty women from twelve countries who design and print textile products which are then sold. Before describing the project in detail let me sketch the context - geographical, historical and sociological - since patterns of migration to Sweden have their own particular characteristics.

Tensta

Tensta, where Livstycket is located, is a suburb about ten miles northwest of central Stockholm. It was built in the late 1960s and consists mainly of blocks of flats, three to eight storeys high, surrounded by trees. For purposes of administration, Tensta originally belonged to a group of six suburbs, five of which differed little in general social profile from the rest of Greater Stockholm. They consisted mainly of older buildings or detached houses inhabited by native Swedes or assimilated immigrants who had been settled in the country since the 1950s. Tensta, on the other hand, was from the start populated by young, recently arrived immigrant families. The median age in Tensta in the 1970s was 28 and it has not changed much since.

Finns originally constituted the largest foreign group; today they are second to the Turks in number. Other groups include (in declining order of population) Iraqis, Ethiopians, Chileans, Iranians, Lebanese, Somalis and Syrians. Altogether, more than 100 languages are spoken by the inhabitants of Tensta.

In the mid-1970s Finns, Greeks and Turks together made up 70 per cent of Tensta's immigrant population. Many of the people from Finland have left since then, among them numerous Finnish Travellers, who have mostly moved to the neighbouring suburb of Rinkeby. In the 1970s, immigrants of all nationalities worked hard and wanted to bring their relatives to join them.

As Swedish statistics define *invandare* (immigrant), it means, 'a foreign citizen settled in Sweden or a Swedish-born resident with at least one parent born abroad'. The percentage of Tensta's population consisting of immigrants has grown over the past quarter century as follows: 1970: 17%;1976: 30%;1986: 40%; 1996: 66%.

In 1996, 42 per cent of Tensta residents received economic assistance from Social Services (the Greater Stockholm figure was 10 per cent); unemployment in Tensta stood at 12.3 per cent (Greater Stockholm, 6.3 per cent); the percentage of residents born abroad was around 66 per cent (Greater Stockholm, 19 per cent).

By 1978 approximately 40 per cent of Tensta's inhabitants had moved out of the suburb. Since then the population has stabilised at about 15,000. However, due to higher birth rates among immigrants, the percentage with foreign citizenship has been growing. Today between 80 per cent and 100 per cent of the pupils in a typical Tensta classroom will have foreign-born parents and a mother-tongue other than Swedish. In Greater Stockholm the equivalent figure is around 16 per cent.

The context - how projects come and go

As people of so many nationalities moved into Tensta, some social problems arose. To help the different ethnic groups adjust to the Swedish way of life, projects of various kinds have been started, some continuing longer than others.

I shall mention a few of the more important ones, which will give you an idea of the needs of the different groups. In every project both the users and providers of services encounter difficulties, which each tries to solve within their own cultural framework. In describing these difficulties as they relate to the various ethnic groups I sometimes generalise and indulge in speculation. I hope this causes no offence. My loose discussion contains many loose ends.

The first large foreign group in Tensta was the Finns, among whom there were many well educated men. There were also many single mothers from Finland, attracted by Swedish society's more tolerant attitude to their situation. Sweden and Finland, like fellow 'Nordic' nations, put few restrictions on the migration and free movement of labour between them. The Swedish labour market was booming in the late 1960s and Finnish men easily found work. Unmarried men often brought their girlfriends over from Finland, and when they had children they saw to it that Finnish-speaking creches were available, and eventually education in Finnish by the state school system. A Project was started for the single mothers to give them economic assistance while they were learning Swedish and being trained as kindergarten teachers

 or nurses. Nearly half of the Tensta Finns who did not return to their own country eventually moved to more prosperous parts of Greater Stockholm. As an ethnic group, Finns in Sweden today are, by and large, quite assimilated.

A Project for Traveller immigrants - serving 250 families from Finland, 100 from Poland and 150 from Spain - was started in 1979 to help preserve the Romany language and cultural heritage. Swedish social policy in the 1970s was to foster cultural identity as essential to successful integration into Swedish society. The Project encouraged Traveller women to acquire reading and writing skills and to send their children to school. Special classes were set up in which the children could speak Romany. A survey showed that most Traveller men wanted to be trained as drivers, car mechanics or horse trainers. The Project backed that training with economic assistance.

However, Travellers tend to keep within their own culture (much like the more recently arrived Somalis). Now and then a Traveller youngster tries to break loose from the kinship system, but this is very difficult. Such matters are discussed at the Romany court, the *Kris*, where the elders' judgement carries great authority.

The Greek presence at Tensta dates from the 1967 Colonels' coup. Greek immigrants in Sweden have always maintained close contact with relatives at home and, in the early years, always expected to go back to Greece some day. The Greeks at Tensta found jobs quickly and made sure their children got a good education. They also kept a close eye on their children's activities. The Greek basketball team Akropolis became one of the best in Sweden. The Greek immigrants also formed societies where democratic ideas were discussed. When the political situation in Greece improved in the 1970s, about a third went back, but some of those have since returned to Sweden. Many Greeks brought their elderly parents to join them in Tensta. In the 1990s a Project called *Kapi* was started to provide a meeting place for the elderly where they could socialise in Greek and have a Greek-speaking doctor available.

The next groups to immigrate were the Turks and the Kurds, who arrived between 1970 and 1985. As it happened, about 70 per cent of the Turks came from the small region of Konya and the village of Kulu. Until 1993, a special bus went between Tensta and Kulu every summer, so those who couldn't manage the trip to Turkey on their own could visit their relatives. Most of the Turkish women were illiterate and few of the men had had much schooling. Despite the official policy that every immigrant should study Swedish at least three hours a day, Muslim traditions tended to keep Turkish women at their chores at home and away from the classroom.

Turkish children of both sexes, however, promptly learned Swedish at school. They could also receive regular lessons in Turkish, since, at the time, all immigrants were entitled to 'home language' instruction. But education was not much encouraged by Turkish parents and not all their children availed themselves of this opportunity. Consequently, second-generation Turks tend to have a limited command of their parents' native language. In this they differ markedly from second-generation Greeks.

In 1979, a report on the Turks of Tensta by a social studies student confirmed what had long been noticed by the social workers, that Turkish families seemed to require more help than other groups. Some examples of their problems were the following: many men had a second wife in Turkey; some young girls were forced to go to Turkey to be married. Others were confined to the house and deprived of all but the legal minimum of education. Both wives and daughters might be beaten if they disobeyed rules set down by their husband or father. A wife who sued for divorce would be completely rejected by her husband's relatives, and often by her own relatives as well. This continues to happen.

A Project was started to encourage Turkish parents to take a greater interest in their children's schooling, but it failed to arouse interest.

In the 1980s narcotics - mainly cannabis and (smoking) heroin - began to pour into Tensta. Some Turkish boys dropped out of school and began to use and sell drugs. The Turkish gambling houses, which are illegal in Sweden, also attempted to recruit young men. Those involved in the gambling clubs often sought to prevent young men from joining the regular Turkish club - for example, the clubhouse was set on fire several times between 1993-95. More recently Muslim fundamentalist leaders have come to Tensta, trying to undermine the authority of the local Imam, who held quite progressive views. After much pressure he was forced to leave.

Of considerable importance was the Kurdish Project, which was in operation from 1984 to 1990. During that time Tensta had the largest Kurdish population of any city in Europe. Kurds and Turks were very hostile towards each other. For example, members of both groups would not let their children attend the same kindergarten. There were two distinct groups of Kurds. One, which had been driven into western Turkey during Ataturk's time, was used to an impoverished life in the countryside. People in this group tended to be uneducated and to have low self-esteem. Under the threat of persecution, they had acquired the habit of concealing their Kurdish identity, something they continued to do after they came to Tensta. The other group had never previously left Kurdistan. The men, often well educated, all considered themselves soldiers in the struggle for a free Kurdistan. Many had been in combat and many had suffered harsh imprisonment. In Tensta they were always discussing politics. Everyone seemed to be in constant touch with events at home. The women for the most part stayed in the background.

The Kurdish Project was funded by Social Services at Tensta and was staffed by a Kurdish lawyer, journalist and physician (specialising in gynaecology) and a Kurdish speaking Swedish psychologist. From the Swedish point of view, the Project's chief aim was to teach the Kurds about Sweden's laws and mores and to facilitate their dealings with the Swedish authorities. But the Kurds wanted it also to function as a central organ of the community, a clearing house for information and source of advice. The Project reached about 150 families. It helped to establish a rehabilitation centre, run by the Red Cross, for victims of torture. It also published a newsletter and two magazines which became internationally known.

Following the murder of prime minister Olof Palme in 1986, there were numerous newspaper articles that placed suspicion on the Kurdish community. Various police investigations of the Kurds led to their increased distrust and fear of the Swedish authorities. Yet when family problems arose (e.g. child-beating), social workers found they could turn to the Project for advice and cooperation. The Kurds from Kurdistan usually planned to return home, and thus had little motivation to become integrated in Swedish society. That was probably part of the reason why the Project, in spite of its success, was forced to close down, as the support of the Social Services was eventually withdrawn.

Meanwhile, the Kurdish Project had served as a bridge between the two cultures. Unfortunately, some of the work it started had to be left unfinished (e.g. the compiling of a Kurdish-Swedish dictionary). Some Kurdish men returned to Kurdistan to fight, leaving their families behind; and some Kurds sent much of their money to Kurdistan. But their children, growing up in Sweden, seem to take little interest in politics. They are losing their sense of ethnic identity, much to the chagrin of their parents.

This kind of rift between parent and child also characterises many of the families from Chile. The strong emphasis this group has placed on maintaining their ethnic identity has resulted in their culture tending to become fossilised - this makes it even harder for the younger generation to accept. Before fleeing from the dictatorship of Pinochet, almost all the Chilean men, and many of the women, had been politically active. They brought their political enthusiasm with them to Sweden. A Project was dedicated to this group, funded, like the others, by the Tensta Social Services. It was called the Latin-American Project and went on from 1978 to 1984.

The purpose of the other Projects had been to strengthen the immigrants' own culture while giving them the opportunity to learn more about the Swedish way of life. But the Chileans were quite critical of some aspects of Swedish life. They insisted they could only accept 'critical (i.e. selective) integration'. They wanted to remain culturally Latin American, intending to return to Chile as soon as possible. At the same time they wanted to influence Swedish society. They would take from the Swedish way of life only those elements they felt were ideologically in accord with their plans for their children's education and upbringing. But many of the children, when they became teenagers, fought shy of parental demands for political engagement. The girls, especially, were eager to enjoy the freedom taken for granted by young Swedes. This was the cause of much conflict.

Another project, *Sandino*, was started, with the aim of exposing at-risk Latin American youths to their home-country's traditional culture via music and theatre. The leaders of *Sandino* choose plays, etc, and hold discussions with the purpose of encouraging the young people to take an interest in politics as well as the performing arts.

When it again became possible, many of these immigrants returned to Chile. Some later came back to Sweden because their children had had difficulty adapting to Chilean life; others because they found themselves not as welcome in the old country as they had hoped.

During the reign of Idi Amin many refugees came from Uganda. They were followed by other Africans - e.g. Gambians and, most recently, Somalis. No project has yet been started for any of these groups, but several have formed their own societies, where old-country traditions are kept alive, especially by the women. Most African born Tensta residents have a high regard for education and encourage their children to speak their mother tongue well. Many of the African women live alone with their children. Political changes (e.g. in Uganda) have enabled many Africans to return home, but few families have chosen to do so.

The recent war in former Yugoslavia produced a wave of refugees, most of whom never intended to remain permanently in Sweden. The majority, moreover, came from cities and were well educated, and this made it relatively easy for them to adjust to the new environment. Many, however, were scarred by the traumas of war and in need of psychiatric care, which was provided in neighbouring Rinkeby, by the Bosnian Project.

Iraqis and Iranians form two other major immigrant groups. No projects have yet been started for either of them, though many Iraqi men receive assistance from the Centre for Victims of Torture. Most of the Iranians are well educated and they have formed self-help societies within their own community.

The following may be some of the reasons why no Project has been started for particular ethnic groups since 1984: lack of funds - state finances are worse than before; growth of unemployment - foreignness is a handicap on the job market; and growing tension between youths from different ethnic groups - both between ethnic minority groups, e.g. Turks against Eritreans, and between Swedish racists (in growing numbers) and all immigrants.

By the 1980s Swedes had become a minority at Tensta. Swedish families were continuing to move away and leaving their place to new immigrants, who were often the relatives of old ones. It was then recognised that integration would never occur as long as immigrants and their children met no other Swedes than teachers and social workers.

A study in the late 1980s described many of the sons and daughters of immigrants as speaking what has come to be called 'Rinkeby Swedish' - the patois of Rinkeby (the neighbouring suburb with roughly the same demographic profile as Tensta). It is easy to hear the difference between it and ordinary Swedish. It is spoken in a staccato rhythm and its vocabulary includes words from Romany and Turkish. 'Rinkeby Swedish' has always made a bad impression on potential employers; and in these times of a large labour pool it has become a virtual disqualification for all but the most menial jobs.

However, despite the present hard times, two Projects have been started recently at Tensta. Both differ from earlier Projects in that they are not ethnically-defined. One is the Järva Ateljén, an excellent art school. Founded in 1989, it is currently attended by 12 pupils, mostly drop-outs between 16 and 22. The other is Livstycket, which was started in 1992.

Livstycket

Many teachers of Swedish for immigrants had noticed that their pupils didn't learn much just by doing homework and coming to class. It occurred to one of them, the art historian Birgitta Notlöv, that the women she taught might learn more if they could combine their studies with practical work. Most of these women knew how to cook and many could sew. She suggested to primary schoolteachers at Tensta that they ask pupils if their mothers would be interested in acquiring sewing skills and learning to print on cloth, in addition to learning Swedish. The first school facilities she arranged for this purpose consisted of three rooms and a kitchen. In August 1992 these became the first Livstycket workshop.

The rooms were small and at first there was no equipment, so Birgitta Notlöv, and her friend Lotte Klein - a designer by profession - borrowed sewing machines. They took home the fabrics they used, to be dyed and washed before beginning the silkscreen printing process, which was done on the premises. The presence of the Swedish-language teacher in the Project meant a second chance for the women who had not been allowed to continue their Swedish studies (the state pays for a maximum of only 800 to 1,000 hours). Many had learned no more than a few words of Swedish at school. Working mainly as charwomen, they had had little opportunity to practise their Swedish.

Birgitta Notlöv presented the new Project to the District Social Committee. They saw its potential and decided, along with two neighbouring districts, to support Livstycket financially and allow the women participating in it to receive social assistance while they were studying. From then on, social workers could inform their clients that they could work and study at the same time by joining Livstycket, and that they could apply to extend their participation in the Project beyond the normally permitted period of a year and a half.

Livstycket was now launched, and its reputation quickly spread. The pupils, who came from many ethnic groups, made their own designs and printed them on cloth. Inspiration was often derived from the flora and fauna of the designer's homeland - or from fruit on the fruit-stand just outside the workroom window. Traditions from both the women's native and adoptive countries influenced their designs. The women also baked bread together and took turns preparing lunch. The different types of bread they baked inspired the designs of tablecloths and napkins; flowers and fruit suggested form and colour for curtains and sheets; various animals - cats, lizards, cows and camels - decorated cloths used for pillows and handbags. Costs were kept as low as possible: e.g. old newspaper was used with the printing screens. No cloth was thrown away, remnants being eventually woven into traditional Swedish 'rag rugs'.

About nine teachers are currently employed in Livstycket, most of them on a part-time basis. A counsellor is also engaged. The 64 women currently participating in the Project speak some 20 different languages. Fifteen of the women come from Chile, fifteen from Arabic-speaking countries (mainly Iraq and Lebanon), five from Eritrea, six from Turkey, four from Somalia, three each from Pakistan, Iran, Uganda and the Gambia and seven from other countries. Here is a simplified picture of the growth of Livstycket:

Aug-Dec

	1992	1993	1995	1997
Pupils	12	20	64	64
Contributions*	61,000	245,000	305,000	990,000
Salaries	37,000	216,000	256,000	480,000
Materials	15,000	79,000	110,000	490,000
Sales	3,700	56,000	203,000	490,000
Admin.	2,700	10,000	108,000	89,000
Rent 3 rooms		342,000 (900 sq.m)	974,000	

*All amounts are in Swedish kroner

Note that from 1993 to 1995 Livstycket increased from 20 to 64 pupils without using many additional teachers. At the same time it moved to larger quarters in central Tensta (as reflected in the larger rent figures). More equipment was also acquired. In short, the workload was becoming too great. Administration costs had been rising too, perhaps not proportionately. Yet sales were booming. Livstycket had been obliged to reject some big orders and it was obvious that with the new, larger workshop, sales could rise even higher. Consequently, Livstycket was changing its status from that of a Project to that of a nonprofit organisation. Its surplus was ploughed back into the running of the operation.

The budget for 1997 is estimated at 4,454,000 Swedish kroner, of which 990,000 consists of contributions from three districts - including Tensta of course.

So far the decision as to which designs should be chosen, printed and put up for sale has been left to Lotte Klein and Birgitta Notlöv. It would be useful to have more teachers in the designing and printing process, but it is not easy to find designers who are content to suppress their urge to make designs of their own to foster the creativity of the women at Livstycket, who are mostly unsophisticated and express themselves in poor Swedish.

Before starting at Livstycket participants are tested and put into one of five Swedish language groups at the appropriate level. According to the Project's internal survey, a quarter of the women are illiterate and another quarter have attended school for only one or two years. Two thirds receive social welfare, and many others receive unemployment benefits. About a third are single mothers. The average number of children per participant is three.

The women spend the first three weeks learning all the various aspects of practical work at Livstycket. Then they begin to follow a schedule, half of which is devoted to theory and half to practical work.

	Monday	Tuesday	Wednesday	Thursday	Friday
T	Swedish Grammar	Reading Swedish Litera-		Maths	Colour, Form, Calligraphy
H	____	ture	Writing (some for the	____	____
E	Own Project	____	magazine)	General Assembly	Civics
O	____	Prepare and present a subject	Poems, childhood memories	____	____
R	Communi- cation	Something read/reflec- tions on own		Guest of the week	Visits- Getting to know
Y		experience			Stockholm

The work day is from 8:30 am to 4:00 pm. Mornings begin with callisthenic exercises done to music. The women prepare their lunch together, Fridays being devoted to Swedish food. A room for prayer is set aside for the Muslim women. The theoretical programme on Tuesdays is led by a professional actor who helps with enunciation. Women may join Livstycket throughout the year, but there is now a waiting list of about 10 to 15 persons.

The main principle of Livstycket is that familiarity with more than one culture is an asset. The goals of its participants are:

♦ To learn Swedish, and become familiar with Sweden and its culture
♦ To learn to express oneself verbally and through art
♦ To gain self-confidence
♦ To develop skills - sewing, drawing, designing, printing, also tending a switchboard and organising exhibitions
♦ To benefit from the work group as a social support network
♦ To learn to accept cultural differences. To learn to discuss, argue, compromise, etc.
♦ To discover one's abilities and try out ideas
♦ To develop a critical eye for art and design
♦ To know the satisfaction of producing quality handicrafts

The beneficial social effects of Livstycket have been quite noticeable. To begin with, the pedagogy of combining theoretical with practical work accelerates language learning. Secondly, working with other women, all of whom are sometimes forced to use sign language, makes for a light mood and sweeps away self-consciousness and feelings of inferiority. Two thirds of the women in Livstycket had never before been in contact with women of other cultures. They had spent most of their lives at home, either alone or with small children. Their husbands, if unemployed, spend their time with friends at cafes or (in the case of the Turks) at the local club, from which women are excluded. Working in Livstycket also gradually increases women's courage to mingle in Swedish society. The children of immigrant families with unemployed parents often act as interpreters between the family and Swedish authorities, sometimes in cooperation with official interpreters. It has been observed that, after a year in Livstycket, women become confident enough to rely on their own grasp of Swedish, or at least on the sole help of the official interpreters. Schoolteachers have also reported to the Social Services that children are proud of their mothers' work in Livstycket, which is displayed in the Project's big shop window on the main street of Tensta.

Livstycket has also been featured in two periodicals - one a magazine devoted to contemporary design. By now it has established itself as a trade name. Since Tensta often appears in the media as an example of failed social engineering, rife with crime, etc, anything that gives the suburb a more positive image is important to its inhabitants. Livstycket also militates against the fossilisation  of culture. The women feel free both to accept each other's influence and to develop their own individual styles. Another benefit it gives the women is an opportunity during the lessons to discuss issues critically, for example Islamic fundamentalism. As already mentioned, fundamentalists from Muslim countries come to Sweden to proselytise. There is pressure to conform to strict Muslim laws regarding women's status and conduct. (In order not to offend any Muslim family the teachers are all female.)

The discussion groups also give some of the women the courage they need to talk to their daughters about sexual matters. In many traditional societies it is often a grandmother or aunt who performs this function. In Sweden, where these relatives may not be available, the subject may never be touched on at all at home, and information about it it is apt to come only from the Youth Advisory Services and the schools. Livstycket also invites professionals to speak about, and encourages discussion of, such topics as female genital mutilation, drugs and family laws.

The Project has also served as a reference group for the City Museum of Stockholm. When the Museum was preparing an exhibition about childbirth, the women of Livstycket provided a display of traditional swaddling clothes.

Another important benefit is that in Livstycket the hierarchy of nationalities breaks down. Whoever deserves credit for a good job gets it. The newly arrived Somalis are, in many respects, a low-status group among immigrants, but not in Livstycket.

The Project has diversified somewhat since 1994. The women who are more interested in cooking than in designing and sewing, for example, can prepare food; and people in the neighbourhood can order food for special occasions from Livstycket. Many are also engaged in writing and printing the Project's newsletter and magazine. Some women like the designing part best, some the printing or sewing. Everybody, after the introductory three weeks, is encouraged to do the practical part she likes best.

It is interesting to observe differences between the ethnic groups in design preference, and in the dynamics of inter-group discussions. Many of the Turks and Iraqis like gold, so a lot of gold colour is used in their designs. They would gladly use shiny fabrics, including synthetics, as well, but Lotte Klein insists on plain, natural materials like linen and cotton.

The Turkish women generally seem to have low self-esteem (or are very modest). After the three weeks of basic study they often volunteer for the most menial jobs, e.g. sweeping the floors, washing the screens. They need encouragement to try designing as well. The designs they do make tend to be small and timid.

The women from Chile often make bold designs and strong patterns, which seem to reflect their greater self-confidence. This was also obvious in the previously mentioned Latin American Project.

The designs made by the Somali women are, from the Swedish point of view, quite exceptional. They are very free in expression and stand out for their originality. One Somali woman explained that she enjoys showing with her designs that her country, which everybody has seen in the news as ravaged by war, can produce flowers and plants of beauty.

How does one recognise the Livstycket style? Successful marketing demands that people know what to expect from Livstycket. Lotte Klein provides the discerning eye here. The designs are not her own, but she looks at each pattern and discusses with the maker how to use it or how to improve it before printing it. A design is never rejected altogether; at least one print is always made from it. But to keep the level of quality on the market high, Lotte Klein and Birgitta Notlov decide what is good enough to be reproduced for sale. Livstycket's products have a reputation for high quality, and are priced accordingly. The Project currently has many orders from libraries, schools and offices, for curtains, table-cloths, etc. One prestigious shop in central Stockholm carries an array of Livstycket products, especially bags and scarves.

Discussion: ethnicity, gender and the host nation

What is the difference, then, between Livstycket and the other Projects in Tensta? Many positive aspects have been mentioned, but what are Livstycket's drawbacks? Does it lack anything important?

The aim of all the previous Projects was principally to integrate immigrants into Swedish society. The immigrant was seen as an asset whose culture ought to have an enriching effect on Swedish culture. Projects therefore aimed to strengthen the minority culture of the immigrants, and the schools were aiming to improve immigrant children's literacy in their mother tongue as well as in Swedish. Swedes, it was thought, should learn to appreciate the diverse cultures around them, and the bearers of those cultures should be proud of their heritage. The various ethnic groups could only affirm themselves if they were strong, and to be strong they needed to maintain their distinct cultural identities.

This type of separatism is no longer considered desirable, and is publicly discouraged, although 'home languages' are still taught in many schools. Immigrants are now urged to assimilate. Swedes are urged to explore their own distinctive culture, increasingly seen as something worth preserving since Sweden's entry into the EUR. To the astonishment of immigrants, native Swedes tend to be hesitant and uncertain when asked to define their national culture. Immigrants of the late 1990s, especially second-generation youths, have begun to challenge the view that only those with native Swedish parents have a right to call themselves Swedes. 'I consider myself Swedish', they say again and again in the schools and the media.

Another characteristic of Projects before Livstycket is that they often encouraged an interest in politics. Many of the people who participated in them were politically active. Livstycket does not concern itself with politics. Emphasising different political views is apt to undermine the bases of communal spirit. In any event, most immigrants of the 1980s and 1990s in Tensta - especially youths - are quite uninterested in Swedish politics.

Livstycket does not do much to help its participants explore their own cultural and linguistic resources. It may put too much emphasis on adapting designs to Swedish taste, since that seems to be necessary for commercial success. Would more risk-taking in design be beneficial? Perhaps there should not be so much stress put on commercial success.

Moreover, the Project does nothing to teach its participants about democracy.

They don't vote for the patterns to be produced; they don't decide the prices; and the products themselves are usually too expensive for them to buy. Many of the women regret and resent this. To this criticism the teachers answer: 'The democratic process is a slow one. We don't have the time'.

Another objection is that Livstycket depends essentially on two individuals, Birgitta Notlöv and Lotte Klein. True, the products have to sell and the buyers are mostly Swedes, so it is important to have someone who can choose designs and colours and materials that Swedes will accept. But this reliance on particular individuals also makes the Project vulnerable.

To make quality products Livstycket needs its highly skilled women. It would like to keep its best workers for a very long time, and this creates a conflict with the Social Services, who want the women off the dependency on welfare payments associated with participation in Livstycket, and into the labour market. The Social Services have to save money and want the women to get paying jobs, but Livstycket wants to keep them and develop their skills.

And there is another difficulty. Sometimes the best workers are needed to work overtime, evenings or weekends, to meet a deadline for an order. But if the women work overtime and get paid for it, that income is deducted from their welfare payment (since welfare is not considered income), so in effect they are working for no pay, and they have no economic motive to put in overtime. The only women in the Project who can benefit economically from overtime are the widows and pensioners, or the few who have taken out State Study Loans. Because of this anomaly Livstycket has had to reject some orders.

Another difficulty is, how should the best workers receive recognition? The printed products, for example, being collective work, are always signed with the trade name 'Livstycket'. This is unfair to some highly skilled workers, but no changes in the policy have yet been planned.

What is the impact of Livstycket on the women's families? The Swedish welfare system has its roots in quite a long tradition. The first people who needed economic support from social welfare were families in which the men were absent or had alcohol problems. It was therefore decided that welfare payments would be made directly to the women, who were considered more responsible. And that is the way it is still done today. When Tensta was young this worked well enough. Most of the men had jobs, and the women either had jobs or stayed home and kept house. But today, while in other parts of Stockholm the gender gap in unemployment is small (men 6.1%; women 5.4%), in Tensta it is large (men 14.9%; women 9.7%). A new situation arises when the husband is unemployed and his wife, who receives both the welfare and child support payments, is also learning a trade at Livstycket. Some men feel their proper role in the home has been taken away, and many feel humiliated.

I know of one extreme case: an elderly Lebanese father of six who made his kitchen (by tradition the woman's domain) into a sort of private fortress. He slept in front of the cooker and decided who could use the kitchen and when.

It was the only way he felt he could retain some sense of control over his family. Another way a man may maintain his self image as breadwinner, and have his own career, is by becoming a dealer in drugs or stolen goods.

It is important to get the men interested in the Project from the beginning. Something very vital is lost when a husband is left out of an important process of growth being experienced by his wife. The Livstycket women are, after all, gaining a certain amount of independence. They are also widening their social network, often beyond the extent of that of their menfolk. After Livstycket many women want to go into business for themselves. But without their husbands' approval and support this is quite impossible for most of them.

There is no forum in which men are encouraged to discuss Swedish life and culture, child-care, relationships, feminism, the changing concept of manhood and fatherhood, democracy within the family, etc - all subjects the women discuss at Livstycket. There are societies and clubs where many men spend a great part of their time, but according to them, talk there doesn't usually deal with 'private matters'. The women are slowly developing a different approach; the men hardly understand what that is. The sad result, as social workers have observed, is that husbands and wives are ceasing to have a common language.

There are many issues facing the Project at present. Livstycket's board of directors have decided to apply for funds from the European Union. Would such support help it to develop new ideas? Would it lead to collaboration with similar projects in other countries?

There are also a number of other questions: the women want wages, not social welfare - can this be managed?; some would like to design, print and sew clothes that they themselves could afford to buy; there is the possibility that Livstycket might have a satellite Project, training women to produce more economical goods; there might also be a satellite Project, or production team, to handle all the big orders; or a catering service could be set up; or a postal order service; or the centre could provide training in entrepreneurship.

Of interest for the future of Livstycket is a budding partnership with a small project in a neighbouring suburb. This consists of a carpentry shop where ten men make wooden furniture. It has already made one prototype of a deckchair, for which the women of Livstycket have produced the cloth parts. Perhaps this first attempt will continue as a joint venture.

I hope it does.

Crossing cultural boundaries

Marginalised children and families in the French school system

Hassan Ezzedine and Alain Grevot

Hassan Ezzedine *and* Alain Grevot *describe a project for schoolchildren in France.*

This paper describes an aspect of the work of a specialist social work team which is part of a non-governmental organisation, *Jeunesse, Culture, Loisirs, Technique* (JCLT). The team, an *équipe de prévention*, is located in a town about 50 miles north of Paris. One of the team's projects, an *accompagnement scolaire*, illustrates work taking place at a crossroads of cultures. These cultural crossroads include: professional cultures - the project promotes joint work between social workers, teachers, youth workers and volutary workers; social cultures - the project takes place in a large area of public housing, and leads to encounters between people of many different socio-economic classes and religious groups; ethnic cultures - the area houses people with roots in many places on the globe.

The work is also taking place in a particular wider socio-economic climate. In France there are about 3 million unemployed people (November 1996), and another 5 million whose employment is precarious. There are cuts in central and local government funding, and there is a crisis over the model of integration which the state promotes. JCLT started work on this project in 1994. Funding is insecure, a series of short term contracts with the local authority, constantly re-assessed and re-negotiated.

The town where the housing estate is located has about 60,000 inhabitants. The city centre is by a small river, and the main public housing estates are on hills to the north and south of the town. We are working on the estate to the south, St Jean. There are about 16,000 inhabitants, of whom 43 per cent are under twenty, and 75 per cent of adults are working class. 86 per cent of the inhabitants are French citizens, but there are 46 ethnic groups represented within the estate. Unemployment is high and St Jean is an 'education priority zone' (National Urban Policy).

Within the estate, people are scattered in many micro-areas, each with a strong identity built up over the past forty years. Mutual mistrust between the inhabitants of micro-areas is high, and one of the aims shared by all professionals working in St Jean is to encourage mutual acceptance between the inhabitants of the different micro-areas.

The JCLT *équipe de prévention* is a specialist community work team which first started working in St Jean in 1987, offering a voluntary and confidential service to parents and children. The team includes four social workers (*éducateurs spécialisés*) and one psychologist.

The project described here was started in 1994. The aim was to develop, in one of the poorest areas of the estate, which is part of a social rehousing programme (PRS), a programme to support children's commitment to school and education. We wanted, working on a voluntary basis, to support and encourage children between the ages of 8 and 14 who were in trouble at school. We were supported by the *département* (equivalent to the county council) which pays one of our salaries, and by the state, which pays the rent of the ground floor flat where we are based. We are open on weekdays (except for Wednesday when there is no afternoon school), from 5.30 to 7.00 pm, and during school holidays for specific sessions.

Our work

We offer individualised support with school work for children who are known by teachers to have difficulties at school, and there is a small follow-up group of about 5 children. We aim to enhance the children's self esteem and give them a greater sense of security, and to restore their commitment to school. We also try to identify the kind of difficulties that the child may have, and, with the team psychologist, we offer the parents and children specialised individual counselling. We work hard with the parents throughout, and try to enable them to take responsibility for following up their children's progress at school.

Our programme is unusual in that it is located outside the school and in one of the poorest parts of the city. Participation is voluntary and the work is clearly separate from the education system, but it is strongly supported by teachers and head teachers. It is implemented with the support of the local social services department, and we have an effective partnership between public and voluntary social services and other members of our local network. However, 'getting in' to our micro-area has not been easy. It was as if we had initially disturbed the privacy of the people who live there. During the first year, we had to cope with aggressive behaviour and our building was defaced.

We are working with children from four different primary schools and one secondary school. Teachers suggest to children in difficulties, who they think might benefit, that they should come and see us. At the same time the teachers give us a list of the children who they think we could help, so that we can take advantage of any opportunity to make contact with them that may occur. Of course not all the children whom the teachers would like us to help come to see us. Once every three months we meet with each of the teachers to assess the impact and effectiveness of our work. Here is an account of the progress of one child:

> Silli is an 8 year old boy whose parents come from West Africa. His father is
> polygamous. Silli was having a lot of problems with reading, and hardly knew
> the alphabet. Our first aim was to help him to relax and to dedramatise his
> problems at school. Every effort that he made was praised and
> congratulated. He joined in all the school holiday sessions that we set up,
> and became more and more committed and lively. Four months after he
> started to come to us he was reading everything that he could lay hands on.

Of course, sadly, there are only a few 'miracles' like that, but, as one head teacher said 'even if many of them make no significant progress, you can help them not to be completely swamped'.

We work with children from 38 families: 7 French, 3 Portuguese, 17 from north Africa (Algeria, Morocco, Tunisia), 7 from West Africa, 2 Turkish, and 2 mixed families (one parent French, the other from Africa or north Africa).

We meet every family to negotiate a written agreement for the participation of their children in the programme. Initially we decided on that course so that the families could know who we were. We needed face to face contact in order to lay the basis for a relationship of trust. We wanted to have an understanding with them, so that we could talk with them about their children without offending their sensibilities. For example:

> The N'Daye family comes from West Africa and one of their daughters is involved in our project. Her mother is clearly more involved than her father in the educational process, because a girl's upbringing is the mother's responsibility. The first time I met Mrs N'Daye, she discovered that I speak one of the Senegalese languages, and she immediately became more confident. As time went on she came to trust us more and more, asking for counselling about her daughter's behaviour, and bringing us Senegalese food that she had cooked.

Seventeen volunteers work with me in the project, mostly women. They are all French, and live outside the St Jean area. Most of them are middle or upper class. Many of them feared meeting people living in the PRS; they were afraid of the bad reputation that the area has, and they were anxious about their role with these very lively children. We had to help them to relax and be at ease when faced with the children. We helped them to think about their own behaviour so that they could avoid anything that might be insensitive towards the children. We set up a methodical and clear process aiming to help them to see other people as they are. We encouraged them to use their natural warmth to gain a place alongside the children.

Most of the volunteers were afraid of making their first contact with the St Jean area and its inhabitants, but no racial or cultural conflict has manifested itself between the children or their parents and the volunteers. One of the volunteers, a midwife, married to a radiologist, told us that her husband was very worried when she said that she was going to work with us. He thought that at the worst she would be raped, and that at the very least, their car would be broken into. There were no problems for her, and she is now proud to tell her middle-class friends how much she enjoys helping these children.

Our programme has been evaluated with teachers, head teachers, education inspectors, social services department social workers, volunteers and members of the county and town councils. We have also included parents. The next step will be to try to decentralise our work, and work with the families in their own homes.

Contextualisation

Establishing this project involved a series of cultural encounters. One of the most important was the encounter between the schools and social workers. For teachers and school inspectors to support an organisation dealing with school matters, but based outside the walls of the school and employing many volunteers, was a sign of an important process of change. To explain this, it is necessary to describe some aspects of the ethos of French schools. For many years the corporatism of teachers and of the civil servants of the *Education Nationale* has led them to oppose any action set up outside the official education system. The French school system is national and centralised. It was built, at the end of the nineteenth century, on a basis of secularity and republicanism. Education is the business of the state, and the French still remember the School War, the battle between the State and the Catholic schools at the beginning of this century. In 1905 the Church was separated from the state in all aspects of public life, and this included schooling. School teachers (whose 'uniform' was a black coat) were called 'the black soldiers of the republic'. The school itself was a fortress, separate from family and neighbourhood, distancing itself from the influences of the family and the environment. It aimed to teach children not only academic subjects, but also republican values, and children were taught to be good republicans. It was a tool, and a successful tool, for the integration of foreigners into French citizenship. It has taken many years for teachers to accept the idea of sharing their mission with other people, whether professionals or volunteers.

The concept of the 'fortress school' is now in difficulties, and the scale of immigration from northern Africa is creating a challenge to French ideology. Teachers are still trained to think that the school should not be influenced by the environment. In this context, building a working relationship with the schools was fundamentally important. Initially we had to work daily with the teachers. We had to explain that our aim was to work with any child in trouble at school, regardless of ethnic background, and that we would work with the children on both their social and scholastic problems. We were able to engage the teachers in this work with us because it supported them in promoting republicanism. However, this approach meant that we were unable to get any funding on the basis of work with specific ethnic groups (and there were problems over producing a leaflet in Arabic).

There were also cultural encounters between different groups of people involved in the project. Firstly between the social workers and the volunteers. Social work is a young profession in France, and does not have the confidence of a well established identity. There is resistance to the idea of working with volunteers. Social workers' first reaction to working with volunteers is often negative; they are afraid for their own professionalism and ethical stance. There is also the view that volunteers might be creating unemployment; in a country with 3 million unemployed, many consider it a priority that some payment should be made for any work done. As has been described, there was also a need to build bridges between the volunteers and the people who they were working with. The middle-class women were afraid of the people in the St Jean area, and lacking in confidence in their ability to help the children there. We aimed to create practical links both between different social classes and with the elected members of the council in order to change their perception of the people of St Jean.

Cultural differences over child rearing also had an impact on the project. In the African families, education was often seen as the woman's business, and our first partners were usually the women in the families. There was more difficulty in building partnership with French families, because there are frequently very poor links between teachers and parents in France. We found that African mothers were often more prepared to get involved.

The development of this project demonstrates the necessity of taking into account a range of cultural and ideological positions. Hassan's knowledge of an African language, and of an African culture, facilitated the development of the work with some of the minority groups. It was just as important that thought was given to the ideological positions of the teachers and the social workers. Without an appreciation of the teachers' relationship to the community, we might not have anticipated the time that would be needed for preparatory work with them. Without an understanding of the perspective of social workers on volunteers, and of middle-class women on the people of St Jean, we could not have worked successfully with the volunteers to enable them to carry out their task.

Looking for the crevices

Consulting with users of mental health services

Helen Morgan

Helen Morgan describes an unusual initiative in user-consultation.

The fact that the world has become fuller than ever of complexity of every kind may suggest at first that that it is harder to find our way out of our dilemmas, but in reality the more complexities, the more crevices there are through which we can crawl. I am searching for the gaps people have not spotted, for the clues they have missed.

Theodore Zeldin, *An Intimate History of Humanity*

A review by the King's Fund of adult mental health services in three West London boroughs for the Health Agency highlighted the need to consult with stakeholders, especially users[1], when planning services. Although the Health Agency had conducted the usual consultation surveys, they accepted the report's view that this had not been substantial or effective. As a result my colleagues and I were approached in January 1995 by the Health Agency to

---

1. Throughout the project, concern has been expressed about the terminology in current use. I am aware that there are objections to the term 'user', but also that an acceptable substitute has not yet been found. I have, therefore, referred to those who have used psychiatric and mental health services as 'users' throughout the chapter for want of a preferable alternative.

find an effective way of engaging service users in each borough.[2] In broad terms the purpose of this project was:

♦ to elicit users' views about current and future mental health services within each of the three boroughs covered by the Trust;
♦ to draw conclusions from this process which could inform strategies for improving involvement of, and collaboration with, service users in general.

Looking for the crevices

The three of us have all worked in adult mental health for some years and have seen changes that included the closures of the large hospitals, the move to care in the community, and the introduction of the purchaser/provider split. Whilst the old system had many flaws, and there was much to be said for the potential of the new, we saw demoralised professionals struggling to manage a system that was under-resourced, finance-led, attacked by the press and in a state of flux and crisis. The system which has been established to contain disturbance was itself disturbed, and inevitably anxiety was rife.

As a system changes from one form to another, what has been a solid structure inevitably develops fissures. These will cause uncertainty and anxiety, but they can also be places where light gets in. Our central question was whether we could perceive cracks in the system as it changed that could be exploited to allow a more radical form of relationship between those who work in a service and those who use it.

We had all had considerable experience of 'user consultation' in the past, but this had been as service providers and had essentially consisted of 'us' (the professionals) asking 'them' (the users), what they thought of what we did. There were varying degrees of response, from the apathetic to the mildly interested to the belligerent. Whilst small adjustments to the service might result from these consultations, it was usually a frustrating experience, never resulting in any fundamental shift in power relationships.

---

2. This project was originally conceived and implemented by myself, Nick Benefield and Phil Russell. Once it was established as an ongoing process I have continued to work as the sole consultant to the user planning-groups. The others have ceased to have direct involvement due to changes in work and location, but continue their interest and support and have adapted many of the original principles to current projects.

Often the process itself quickly became institutionalised, and rarely did it feel that staff and clients were in any sort of genuine partnership. Those dependent on the service are unlikely to rock the boat too much and those not using it are rarely asked. User consultation conducted by providers is valuable and should retain a place, but it has its limitations.

What interested us about this project was the fact that it was to be a piece of work conducted on behalf of the purchasers rather than the providers, and that it would be borough-wide rather than confined to one particular service. Could it be run as a way of offering a genuine challenge to the status quo? We were particularly concerned to establish if the funders were prepared to move from consultation to partnership and whether they would attempt to find ways of embedding the collaborative process into their systems.

The key figures in the Health Agency responsible for purchasing mental health services seemed keen to find a way of bringing users into the system as more than passive recipients of treatment. Whilst they held many of the purse strings, they were aware that they had difficulty reaching the people on whose behalf they were spending money. The notion of forming a genuine link between themselves and the users had its attractions, and they have remained committed to this process throughout, both by funding the work and in attending all meetings when requested to do so by users.

Power and the status quo

Having made it clear that we were concerned to facilitate a change in relationship from mere consultation to one of collaboration and partnership, we recognised we were proposing a shift in the existing power relationship between provider and user. In planning the project, therefore, we focused on where power had lain historically and where it seemed to be moving in the current system. The following is necessarily a simplistic and brief overview of two important strands.

The Medical Model: Traditionally the medical model has been dominant in the definition and treatment of people with mental health needs. Rooted in physical medicine, the same fundamental precepts pertain when translated to disorders of the mind. The individual under consideration is defined as 'the patient' who is 'ill'. The origins of this illness are regarded as primarily organic and, therefore its treatment is regarded in the same light. The doctors who are trained in such treatments are 'well', and their job is to diagnose the illness and find its cure.

However, unlike most other branches of medicine, psychiatry has been consistently unsuccessful in developing these 'cures'. Medication may help to contain and subdue the more extreme symptoms of the defined illness, but the cost in terms of side-effects can be high and it is rare for the individual to be rid entirely of the original problem. In the process of treatment, the assumptions underlying this model perpetuate a relationship whereby the doctor retains ultimate power and responsibility, thus removing from patients authority over key aspects of their lives. Given that such authority is a central feature of mental health, the model can be viewed as working against its stated aims of helping sufferers to recovery.

The Contract Culture: The introduction of the purchaser/provider split has brought a different authority into the system - that of the marketplace. This is fraught with its own paradoxes and difficulties but also, perhaps, some potential.

Within capitalism, business relies on the existence of customers with money who wish to buy what is produced. The working of market forces assumes that a variety of products is available for selection and the customer will choose that which they prefer and can afford. A company making shoddy, over-priced or unwanted goods will fail whilst others succeed. The 'good' becomes strong, and what is strong survives, so what survives must be good. There is, of course, a range of criticisms of such a system that suggests that, even in the field of commerce, it doesn't exactly work like that. But it is a system and is consistent to some degree within its own context.

However, when you import such an ethos into a service sector such as mental health provision, impossible anomalies occur. By definition, most of those who need the services haven't the money to buy them. The 'punters' have no cash and therefore have no direct power to affect what is made available to them. Purchasing departments are set up to buy on their behalf and are under pressure to spend with care and sparingly. 'Good' services can too easily become those that are cost-effective (or cheap).

The increased pressure for accountability has had its positive effects in forcing organisations to address what they are funded to do, whether they are effective, and tighten up on sloppy practice. However, a central difficulty remains. These institutions exist to serve distressed, human beings and consequently the work is often messy, chaotic, unmeasurable and distressing. Where the emphasis is on cost-effectiveness, it is hard to justify the time required for the building of relationships and the temptation is to go for the short, sharp solution.

Purchasing departments, often staffed by people with little direct experience of mental health work, struggle to meet the requirements from government, whilst uncertain about what it is they are trying to do. The fundamental contradiction is that, however well-meaning the individuals in these purchasing departments are, they are not the ones who will use what they buy and are usually separated from those who will. We have a split customer.

An alternative to the medical model?

In considering the emerging scenario, our interest was in whether there was potential in the change and, in particular, how the entry of market forces onto the scene might alter existing power structures. Health Trusts now have to compete with other service providers and are having to offer ways of working outside of the hospital setting. If there is an easing of the grip of the medical model, can we find something constructive in the philosophical uncertainty remaining?

Each of us had worked in therapeutic communities, and retained a commitment to the movement's philosophical ideals despite its fall in popularity in recent years. These ideals offered a challenge to the medical model by positing a spectrum of health/illness rather than a clear-cut divide. This challenge to the notion of a clean division between the 'ill' patient and the 'well' practitioner leads to a different way of thinking about the relationship between professional and client. The focus of 'treatment' within this model moves from 'cure' to the individual's gaining help in managing their own lives, and places relationships (especially that with the group) at the centre. It requires an acknowledgement of the 'illness' that may arise within the staff group, and a recognition and encouragement of the 'wellness' in the client. It is a difficult task for there is an investment by both client and practitioner to maintain the divide, so that clients can give up the responsibility for being 'well' and practitioners can avoid facing any 'illness' in themselves.

The four aspects of the therapeutic community proper as defined by Rapoport are communalism (the importance of individual and group relatedness), democratisation (the sharing of power regarding decision-making), permissiveness (the toleration of a variety of behaviours but within set limits) and reality confrontation (the presentation to the individual of the effects of their behaviour on others).[3] All these aspects depend on the belief that all members of the community, whilst having to manage personal mental health difficulties, also have the capacity to engage with others, to be well.

Therapeutic communities are usually restricted to a physical building. What happens if the philosophy is shifted outside such confines and applied to a community within a geographical location to form a 'therapeutic community *in* the community'? What sort of relationship between professional and client needs to develop which works to contain the illness and focus on the health of the client? How might individual users be supported so that they are able to manage the process themselves? What then becomes the professional's role and responsibility in facilitating this difference in relationship?

Certain key elements seemed essential in setting up a project if it were to model different ways of relating to and working with users:

◆ The project needed to be established in such a way that it was user-led from the start so that the users involved had a real - not token - say in the running of the project (democratisation). Working as a group together (communalism) was central.

◆ As the 'professionals' facilitating this process, our own 'illness' (including anxiety, need for control, personal tensions, etc) needed to be owned and contained.

◆ A degree of tolerance of the difficulties individuals might experience (permissiveness) was needed, but where someone's behaviour adversely affected others this might need challenging (reality confrontation).

We decided to run a series of search conferences in each borough, organised and run by a group of users who would be paid for their work at a realistic rate. Our role was to establish and facilitate the planning groups, and to act as a link between the service user planning-group and those commissioning the project.

---

3. R.N. Rapoport, *Community as Doctor: New Perspectives on a Therapeutic Community*, Tavistock Publications, London 1960.

Four stages of the project

1. Initial Research

This was to establish basic understanding of the way services were organised, general issues and practices related to user involvement in the area. We were also seeking out ways of making contact with users in the area who would be interested and able to join a planning group.

In all three boroughs there were considerable numbers from ethnic minorities and, although specific services were provided, the consultation system had been little used by them. We decided, therefore, to set up a cross-borough group to consult with users from black and other ethnic minorities.

2. Planning

Having established a general picture, we then identified a group of users in each borough (between 5 and 10) to work with us towards setting up appropriate consultation events. We wrote a job description and criteria and spread these around as much as possible, inviting volunteers to contact us. The usual questions of representativeness arose, but realistically the goal was to identify any user willing and able to support the scheme, and to try to ensure that a representative group of users attended the conferences.

The fact that we were paying users made a significant difference: a) it was a direct incentive to be involved and helped overcome some early scepticism; b) it encouraged users to treat their involvement in a business-like fashion, like a job; c) it made them feel valued and valuable.

Nevertheless, a great deal of scepticism about the genuineness and likely effectiveness of this consultation process existed. Users felt they had been asked to give their views many times over the years, but what they said seldom made much difference. They had a sort of 'consultation burn-out'. As their capacity to network and enthuse others about the process was central to the project, generating enthusiasm required a good deal of explanation and honesty.

We spent far more time on this stage than we had budgeted for, but it was worth it. In each borough it was evident how little users understood about how the system was financed and organised. Whilst the structure of how their services were to be provided had undergone major changes, no one had explained it to them. We spent a considerable amount of time with each group defining the purchaser/provider split, care in the community and the differences between Health Agencies, Health Trusts and Social Services. These sessions underlined how, if any consultation process is to be effective, it must include a first stage of education. The importance of this work was obviously recognised as each group decided to include a similar instruction session at the start of each user conference.

After these initial sessions, each planning team met several times to define the conference programme and organise all the details of the conference. Inevitably, as in any group of individuals working together to plan an event, there were differences of views about how things should be, not everyone always liked each other, and at times there were conflicts and clashes which had to be managed within the group.

The second area we spent time on was that of training the members of the planning teams to develop skills in public speaking, chairing, facilitating, recording in groups, etc. We ran a cross borough training day. These joint meetings, as well as the planning sessions, helped to develop individual confidence and competence, but also gave people whose experiences often leave them feeling isolated and vulnerable a sense of connection and collective strength, a community that both supported and enabled people.

When the outline for the event had been decided upon and the publicity material produced, the groups went out networking. The planning teams identified places where users would meet and went to speak to groups. They achieved a level of contact, loyalty and trust from people who use mental health services which could never be commanded by any group of professionals.

3. The User Events

These events were certainly unlike any other conference we had attended. The prevailing themes were chaos, energy, creativity, and realism. A room full of people with varying degrees of mental health needs at varying stages of health or ill-health can be an unpredictable environment. The user-facilitators were undoubtedly anxious about their new roles and we had a 'run-through' immediately before the doors opened. When the events began, things seldom ran smoothly; timetables slipped and conference organisers with their newly-acquired chairing and recording skills struggled to contain the mass of views that poured forth once participants realised that there were no professional providers present, that the event was being managed by users, and that others were genuinely interested in what they thought. A wide cross-section of people attended. The energy and passion from the membership was exciting and a privilege to share in, and it gradually focused into a range of highly positive and creative ideas.

There was anger, cynicism and resentment expressed, but it did not turn into the kind of destructiveness and negativity that can bedevil even the most sophisticated and highly controlled conferences. There was a realistic understanding of the political, social and financial context, and an honest recognition that the services were vital. Yet alongside this recognition was a frank appraisal of the limitations and shortcomings of these services. People were keen to forge alliances and partnerships with professionals. They were ready to acknowledge the skills and experience of the professionals. Could the professionals, in turn, acknowledge the unique skills, insight and understanding that had been gained at great personal expense by service users in the process of their careers as psychiatric casualties?

4. Feeding back

After each event, the notes taken by planning-group members were gathered together and a report written. The first draft was always discussed among the planning teams and a final draft agreed. This was then distributed to all users who had attended and copies were sent to the purchasers and all providers in the borough.

The reports from each borough event were specific to that locality, but some prevailing themes were striking:

◆ We had been warned that, if asked, users would always demand more counselling for which little money was available. In fact, whilst there was indeed a call for more to be provided in the way of 'talking cures', the strikingly consistent theme was the wish for relationship. The commonest experience recounted was of 10 minutes with a psychiatrist who moved on every six months or so, visits from a variety of community psychiatric nurses, and a vacuum where the social worker used to be. Many knew little or nothing about care plans and they frequently had no idea who their keyworker was supposed to be.

◆ Where they did come into contact with staff, especially in hospital, the experience too often described was of being treated with disrespect and in a patronising manner. Good experiences were recounted, but so too were ones of abuse. Participants recognised the stress on staff as well as the process of institutionalisation which could result in exacerbating the terror that the individual can experience when under section. A solution was sought in users becoming more involved in the training of staff at an early stage in their careers, when they might still be open to an empathic approach to patients.

◆ A worrying feature of the events was the extent of the feelings of powerlessness and fear that emerged. The anxieties expressed, and the need for reassurance that speaking up would not put them personally at risk, was too common to be put down merely to individual paranoia. People who have experienced sectioning, ECT, and having to take medication they haven't chosen or understand, know what it is like to be subject to the power of the system and of another. When recounting their experiences, participants understood the ill state they had been in at the time and how alarming this might have been for others. However, the way some of those in authority had managed this, and the legacy of fear this left, was disturbing.

◆ A contributory aspect of this powerlessness was the lack of information given to users. Few knew much about the system they were in. There was a consistent call for better education for users concerning medication and its side-effects, as well as the opportunity for greater self-management.

◆ There was a consistent complaint that the system was run for the convenience and benefit of professionals rather than for the clients, resulting in the 9 to 5 nature of service provision outside of the hospital. A need for more extensive crisis services was emphasised in all conferences.

◆ Time and time again came a strong and consistent call for the system to shift in order that the users themselves could have a greater say in how services were run. 'We may be ill but we're not stupid', was a common statement. The plea was to involve the people who knew the services from the inside to help spend the money most efficiently.

User/professional events

Up to this point it was we who had provided the bridge between users and professionals. Now the planning teams and the conference participants wanted a direct communication where purchasers and providers were invited to respond to the initial report. Because the report and the conference was sanctioned and commissioned by the purchasers, there was a commitment from senior representatives from Social Services, the Health Trust and the Health Agency to attend.

Again the conferences were organised and facilitated by the user planning teams. In a typical conference, key professionals were invited to respond to sections of the report to the large group. The second part of the conferences consisted of small groups on specific areas of concern, with reports back to the large group. In the final discussions the central issue was how the process of user involvement in the decisions about the running of services would get embedded into the structure.

Outcomes

As this is an ongoing process, it is hard to be definite about the outcomes in terms of real changes to service provision, especially as these varied from borough to borough. At the time of writing, two of the three boroughs have had two further conferences where professionals have been pressed regarding the promises that had been made previously. In both boroughs, the process of involving users in the selection and training of staff is under way, as are structures for user participation in decision-making and planning. A User Liaison post is already established in one borough and proposals for a similar post in the other two are under consideration. A two-day workshop on developing training skills for users has been run, and a group of user-trainers are establishing themselves to develop a training co-operative. In the third borough, as in the cross-borough black users group, things are moving more slowly.

An outcome which is harder to measure is the effect the conferences themselves may have had in lessening the anxiety of professionals concerning working with users and shifting attitudes . It was always a service user in the chair, with the responsibility and authority to manage a group which included senior directors of Social Services, the Trust and the Agency. This meant that the conferences themselves modelled a way in which the balance of authority can alter without dire consequences.

Our role

Throughout this process, our role in facilitating the planning teams was a critical one which we needed to keep under close review. It is often difficult to surrender the control traditionally held by professionals and accept that, although the process may be different, the outcomes unfamiliar and sometimes (in our eyes) flawed, it is necessary to allow people the freedom to develop their own solutions to problems. However, the wish to move from a position where we take too much responsibility, evoking dependency and resentment, can lead to moving too far in the opposite direction so that we become neglectful of users' genuine needs. Finding the correct mix between support and empowerment was always a complex balancing act and there were times when we got it wrong. As the project progressed, the planning groups became more able to tell us when they required our specific skills, and when we should back off.

Conclusion

Whilst this project has not been perfect, there have been substantial achievements both in the specifics of service provision and in the general culture in some areas. The key factors of particular significance where there has been success include:

◆ The project was commissioned and funded by the purchasers rather than the providers. This meant there was the possibility of bringing together the two elements required if the ethos behind market forces is to have any meaning: the people with the money to buy, and those who need and use services. This way a sort of *composite customer* was established, with us as the link. To continue to be effective into the future, this link is being formalised so that the relationship can be a direct one without the need for facilitators.
◆ Whilst this facilitation role was required to form the link, it was important that we were independent of the service provision. This independence allowed for the necessary degree of trust in us to be established by both sides of this new partnership, the purchasers and the users. Where suspicion

has been expressed, this has tended to come from providers. Within the triangle of purchaser, user and provider, where a partnership develops between the first two the third has to move to a different position which may feel uneasy and uncertain. Such suspicion is therefore understandable.

◆ The commitment of the Health Agency to the project allowed the space and time necessary for such work. A common shortcoming of attempts by professionals to consult with users is that the pace is too quick. In their own busy, pressurised, diary-dominated lives, professionals become frustrated by the time it takes to genuinely inform people not used to being told things, to generate optimism in a climate of failure, and to work with the particularities of the mental health problems experienced by the people whom they apparently wish to shift from patients to partners. In response to this frustration, they often withdraw and call the experience a failure; at best a failure acknowledged as born of their own limitations, at worst as evidence that users are incapable of acting responsibly and should therefore continue to be recipients of treatment rather than partners in a process of collaboration.

Because of the unique position we were in, we were able to take the time to build the relationships necessary for collaboration. This is a two-way relationship and time was therefore needed, not only to help and facilitate the development of capabilities in the thirty or so users with whom we worked directly in the planning teams, but also to consider ourselves as the other side of the equation. This has meant facing some difficult truths about our own fears, prejudices and anxieties, and to learn to trust the users themselves to help us manage the process.

This essay will be published later this year in a collection entitled Chaos and Containment in the Community: Social, Systemic and Psychoanalytic Perspectives, *edited by A. Foster and V. Z. Roberts and published by Routledge.*

Innovation through training

Challenges and changes in Italian community psychiatric care

Margherita Gobbi, Monica Savio, Angelo Cassin

The authors show how training processes can themselves be generators of change.

Psychiatric reform

In 1978 Law 180, known as the Italian Psychiatric Reform, required the deinstitutionalisation of mentally ill people and the replacement of psychiatric hospitals with alternative community care structures. During the 1960s, before Law 180 was passed, the de-hospitalisation movement (*'psychiatrica demotica'*) had developed through the work of Franco Basaglia, who had started to run down the psychiatric hospital in Gorizia (Northern Italy). The movement spread from the medical field to mainstream society, joining the wave of cultural and political change brought about by the student movement, the working-class strikes and the fight for women rights. During the 1970s the Abortion Law and the Divorce Law were enacted. The achievement that this represented in terms of civil rights can be understood by considering that Italy is a 99 per cent catholic country, hosting the Vatican State.

The change in the psychiatric care system did not take place in Italy because of the welfare crisis, as in other European countries. It actually represented a particularly innovative way of implementing a particular welfare philosophy, supported by a cultural and political climate in which the left wing parties had joined to fight against marginalisation and social exclusion.

In the psychiatric field the main challenge was, and to a large extent still is, that of providing on a community basis the full range of assistance, medical and social care for people who have left the hospitals. Homelessness is the word that perhaps in English best expresses the fear of the consequences of deinstitutionalisation, and was used in Italy by those who opposed the closure of psychiatric hospitals.

'Senza tetto'

Interestingly enough, there is not an equivalent to 'homelessness' in the Italian language. The literal translation would be *'senza tetto'* - without roof - which is normally used to indicate people who have been left without a home as a consequence of natural catastrophe (earthquake, flood). Possibly the word 'roof' is used in place of 'home' because in Italy the roof is identified with protection, something above one's head providing cover. Thus, speaking about the good qualities of psychiatric hospitals, we would say 'at least it used to provide a roof'. What might be missing then is protection. A home is something that neither psychiatric hospitals nor community care can provide. A home is the result of a personal undertaking, aimed at building an affective structure in one's own life; people can be supported in this process but not provided with a ready made home. Culturally and symbolically, a home represents a life project - Italians are in fact much more home stable than English people. Once Italians succeed in building or buying their 'home', it is very rare for them to move, just as it is also rare to change your job; you have your home and your job for life.

This may be a psychosocial explanation of why 'homelessness' is not as common a word in Italy as in the UK, and is much less often associated with people who have been discharged from psychiatric hospitals. Specifically, being 'homeless' - *'senza tetto'* - is associated with the lack of protection of the person who is experiencing this condition. It is not, as it tends to be in the British case, associated with the lack of protection experienced by society as a consequence of people being homeless; that is, the fear of violence.

The key phrase used by the new community psychiatry is 'therapeutic continuity'. This has to be guaranteed to the mentally ill people on a 24 hour basis for seven days a week. Therapeutic continuity is therefore aimed at providing protection, a symbolic roof which represents a space where someone can experience acute crisis or find some rest from the stresses of their life. Therapeutic continuity and assistance on a 24 hour basis does not necessarily imply residentiality, but only the chance to use it when in need. This is the rationale for providing a limited number of beds on a 24 hour basis (in addition to the beds in psychiatric wards, this provides an average of 15 beds to every 200,000 inhabitants.)

An accessible community service aims both to provide care and assistance for an extended period and to offer a wide range of services for mental health needs. The new psychiatric care philosophy was supported by Law 180, which required that no new psychiatric hospital admission should take place after December 1980, and that compulsory admission could take place only in district general hospitals, for a maximum of seven days and with the permission of two doctors and the mayor of the town where the client is resident.

Asylums without walls

Looking for alternative ways of dealing with clients' needs was an aim of the Psychiatric Reform. The ambitious ideal project was to replace the full time protection of the asylum's walls with the symbolic walls (roof) of social integration. New solutions had to be found within the community care structures, one of which was preventive work aimed at avoiding the need for hospital admission. The alternative way to answer the client's need for 24 hour care was the establishment of '24 hour centres' within the community services. Such structures usually have a very limited number of beds and provide a space for clients' crises, where clinical, social and relational needs can be addressed.

24 hour centres are unfortunately more expensive than day centres, require specific staff training, and are constantly threatened by the possibility of a shift towards a hospital medicalised model rather than a community holistic one. 24 hour centres represent a resource for care in the community, yet at the same time represent a risk of institutionalisation through the establishment of a small asylum in the community. The professional challenge is therefore that of resisting

the temptation to transform the provision of protection on a 24 hour basis into residential care.

The present paper focuses on two problems; first, the crisis of the welfare state is such that economic resources for 24 hour centres are becoming very limited; second, the appeal of the hospital model is reinforced by the employment of workers who have not been sufficiently well trained in the community approach to be able to maintain and establish the care network within the community. There is obviously a risk that the 24 hour centres will become miniature hospitals, within the community, with few resources and little consideration of the continuity of care in the community, thus negating the very rationale for which they have been established.

'Aziendalizzazione' - the welfare market in Italy

Recent changes in the organisation of health care are prompting new developments in the psychiatric field and inevitably affecting the professional culture of community care. Since the 1970s and 1980s the overall structure of the health care system has changed and in some instances become less flexible to the needs of community care. The Italian 'aziendalizzazione' is a movement similar to the UK split between purchaser and provider. The main and most visible consequence of such development is that psychiatric services are now represented on a regional and provincial basis by a Department of Mental Health (MHD). Budgeting has been introduced as a means of organising community and hospital care. Indirectly this has created the need to evaluate care provision in order to negotiate the MHDs' budgets. In many regions budgeting has been linked to objectives. In practice this implies the need for a clear statement of the MHD's objectives in terms of care provision and expected results. Funds should in theory be regulated by the ability of MHDs to demonstrate their care outcomes.

The introduction of economic criteria in the organisation of mental health care has had a significant impact on the everyday life of community centres. Professionals feel less safe, although there is no clear threat to their posts. The limitation of resources and their allocation according to care outcomes is perceived as a constraint and as a direct criticism of their skills. At present there is a considerable level of confusion as to what should be evaluated and how. There is a danger that mental health care will be considered as similar to other medical fields, whose evaluation is relatively simple and clear cut. The evaluation of rehabilitative work is, for example, a challenge that cannot be easily taken up by quantitative techniques. The time needed for rehabilitation to produce results is regulated by individual user's needs and life situation, whereas a successful surgical intervention can be evaluated immediately.

Thus the shift towards more medically oriented patterns of mental health care may be substantially supported by the '*aziendalizzazione*' movement, whose preference for using quantitative criteria to evaluate the provision of care can be used as a professional coping strategy for dealing with the uncertainty of qualitative indicators of the care process. There is then a risk that what is considered 'clinical' in the mental health field becomes purely medical, losing its integration with the social and psychological components.

Training in a time of change

We now want to consider as a case study a training experience in a 24 hour centre. The training took place at the same time as the introduction of the '*aziendalizzazione*', and therefore provided a good opportunity to observe the professionals' experience of change and their use of different coping strategies.

The context is a 24 hour centre in Northern Italy, with a team of 13 registered nurses, 3 auxiliaries, 1 psychiatrist and 1 psychologist. The service has six beds for residential users (day & night hospital facilities) and day centre facilities for clients who are not residential. In order to establish the training content and programme, a number of meetings were undertaken with the staff, with the aim of understanding training needs and requirements. During these meetings the organisational structure of the service was analysed in order to put the training course into context. It emerged as a highly hierarchical organisation, with nurses consistently subordinated to the psychiatrist's hegemony. Overall the service appeared to be mainly medically oriented; nurses had little mental health knowledge or experience of community psychiatric care. Staff morale was low, as the successes and failures of their care were never discussed. The whole organisation was more orientated to

'Introducing economic criteria into the organisation of mental health care had a significant impact on community centres'

professional separation than to a team-work approach. The nursing rota system was such that little time was spent together in planning the care and discussing its development.

The training course was exclusively addressed to the nurses in order to offer them a space in which to talk freely about their professional needs and experience, as well as to become a more powerful professional group in terms of their own perception of their identity and their ability to negotiate and develop their own interventions.

The training structure was made up of 9 meetings of 3 hours each. In each of the meetings two speakers (a nurse and another mental health professional) gave a paper about community rehabilitation theories, crisis intervention models, social networks building, care plan evaluation and social co-operation. The papers were followed by one hour group discussion (small group) and one hour plenary session. The aim was to link theory to practice, both through the speakers who were all experienced practitioners, and through group work. The organisational aim of the service was to prevent the revolving door syndrome, and this entailed discussion of failures in service provision so that plans could be made for future success.

The whole training course was organised with very restricted resources, as the training budget was very limited, and most of the speakers were from the Department of Mental Health to which the 24 hour centre belongs.

The training aimed also at developing critical thinking among the nursing staff by providing: (a) the mental health background that was lacking from their general nursing training: (b) comparative examples of different practice; (c) an understanding of the general organisation where the service was placed and of the community network as a means of tapping into informal care resources which could compensate for the lack of funds and prevent the revolving door syndrome.

In terms of outcome, this training experience has proved to be successful in a number of ways:

◆ nurses in the 24 hour service have become more vocal through realising that their role in the care process is not simply that of providing clients with guardianship during times of crisis. As a result the nursing staff have asked for a change in their rota system in order to create time for team meetings during which they can plan the care project together and monitor its development. Nurses have thus started to develop a new professional culture which is specific to the psychiatric context where they operate.

◆ Carers have positively acknowledged the training initiative by sending a letter to the Director of the Department of Mental Health in which their appreciation of a change in the nursing approach is shown.

◆ At the organisational level, the position of the psychiatrist and of the nurse manager has become openly antagonistic to that of the change-promoting nursing group. This demonstrates that the movement towards privatisation is often a powerful vehicle for enforcing a medically centred approach to psychiatric community care. In such an approach, the emphasis is prevailingly on the diagnostic aspects of mental distress and on the control of symptoms, thus using categories of care which can be easily monitored and which reduce anxiety for professionals. What is forgotten, however, is that a 24 hour centre is part of a care structure whose core is integration with community services, and not separation from them. The integration of services goes hand in hand with the integration of different professional contributions. The transformation of a 24 hour service into a residential building with closed doors can be interpreted as a defensive strategy by those who feel that their professional identity is threatened by community services.

◆ From the trainers' perspective, a new issue has now arisen as to whether to support the nursing group by directly engaging in changing the organisation, openly opposing the supremacy of the psychiatrist, or whether to step back and maintain a neutral position.

At times of significant organisational changes, training intervention cannot but be directed towards an 'action training' approach aimed at supporting the re-definition of both the structure of services and the role of professionals. The meaning of professional action is not separate from perceptions of professional roles and identities, nor from the philosophy which links and makes sense of service strategies.

The politics of care

The Italian experience shows that, when social issues are at stake, psychiatric care cannot be considered as neutral professional ground, neatly defined by care models, plans and evaluation. Professional culture is no more immune to political involvement than psychiatric care in the community. Becoming politically engaged, in this context, implies abandoning the safety of professional neutrality, both that of the trainer and that of the trainees. Thus, the development of the welfare state, the welfare crisis and the re-birth of old medical models connect to changes in the professional culture of those who are institutionally in place to provide care. Should such care and its organisation be considered 'neutral' because 'scientific' or 'political' because of the implications for social and health choices as well as people's civil rights? This seems to be indeed a matter of 'cultures', those of professionals, of users and carers, of administrators, of trainers and trainees.

Changes in culture at one level (the '*aziendalizzazione*') affect structures at another level (the 24 hour service), and bring about changes in the culture of the service. The ideologies of '*aziendalizzazione*' and '*psychiatrica demotica*' are opposed, and when the process of '*aziendalizzazione*' reaches the mental health services a conflict is created which plays itself out within the mental health service team. The shift in the culture of the service towards a scientific/ commercial discourse leads to a hierarchisation of professional identities. The intervention of the trainers, by providing time and encouragement for reflection, acts as a catalyst, reinforcing the identity of the nursing staff, and then brings about a challenge not just to the power of the psychiatrist and the nursing manager, but to the scientific and commercial culture of the '*aziendalizzazione*'.

Soundings

Soundings is a journal of politics and culture. It is a forum for ideas which aims to explore the problems of the present and the possibilities for a future politics and society. Its intent is to encourage innovation and dialogue in progressive thought. Half of each issue is devoted to debating a particular theme: topics in the pipeline include: The European Left, Windrush Echoes and The Concept of Care.

Why not subscribe?
Make sure of your copy

Subscription rates, 1998 (3 issues)

INDIVIDUAL SUBSCRIPTIONS: UK - £35.00   *Rest of the World - £45.00*

INSTITUTIONAL SUBSCRIPTIONS UK - £70.00   *Rest of the World - £80.00*

Please send me one year's subscription starting with Issue Number _____

I enclose payment of £ _____

I wish to become a supporting subscriber and enclose a donation of £ _____

I enclose total payment of £ _____

Name _____

Address _____

_____

_____ Postcode _____

Please return this form with cheque or money order payable to Soundings and send to:

Soundings, c/o Lawrence & Wishart, 99A Wallis Road, London E9 5LN